10

MINUTE GUIDE TO

LONG-TERM RETIREMENT PLANNING

by Mark Battersby

Macmillan Spectrum/Alpha Books

A Division of Macmillan General Reference
A Simon and Schuster Macmillan Company
1633 Broadway, New York, NY 10019

International Standard Book Number: 0-02-861180-2
Library of Congress Catalog Card Number: A catalog record of this publication is available through the Library of Congress.

98 97 96   8 7 6 5 4 3 2 1

Interpretation of the printing code: the rightmost double-digit number is the year of the book's first printing; the rightmost single-digit number is the number of the book's printing. For example, a printing code of 96-1 shows that this copy of the book was printed during the first printing of the book in 1996.

Printed in the United States of America

Note: Reasonable care has been taken in the preparation of the text to ensure its clarity and accuracy. This book is sold with the understanding that the author and the publisher are not engaged in rendering legal, accounting, or other professional service. Laws vary from state to state, and readers with specific financial questions should seek the services of a professional adviser.

The author and publisher specifically disclaim any liability, loss of risk, personal or otherwise, which is incurred as a consequence, directly or indirectly, of the use and application of any of the contents of this book.

Publisher: Theresa Murtha
Development Editor: Debra Wishik Englander
Production Editor: Michael Cunningham
Cover Designer: Dan Armstrong
Designer: Barb Kordesh
Indexer: Becky Hornyak
Production Team: Heather Butler, Angela Calvert, Christine Tyner, Christy Wagner

CONTENTS

INTRODUCTION

This guide is aimed at those under the age of 40. It is designed to provide the tools you need to reach that all-important goal of a financially secure retirement.

As you begin planning for retirement, you will face a tremendous number of decisions. You will learn about the benefit options offered by your employer and things you might not know about your personal finances. You will also learn about the stumbling blocks that may be thrown in your way by family emergencies, unexpected unemployment, and income tax rules. These factors make planning for retirement especially difficult.

The *10 Minute Guide to Long-Term Retirement Planning* will teach you the basics of retirement planning and the investment strategies you can employ to reach your goals. The lessons in this book will guide you through the complexities of employee benefit programs, tax rules, and the many investment options available to you.

You will learn about basic stock, bond, and mutual funds you may already be slightly familiar with, and you will learn about more exotic investments. You will also learn the strategies you can employ to help you reach your retirement goals using all types of investment vehicles.

CONVENTIONS USED IN THIS BOOK

Each lesson will take about 10 minutes or so for you to complete. To help you progress through the lessons, the *10 Minute Guide to Long-Term Retirement Planning* uses the following elements to emphasize important information:

Plain English. Defines new or unfamiliar terms in "plain English."

These are ideas that will help you avoid confusion, or tell you a clever idea.

! This element will highlight common problems you may face, and tell you ways to avoid them.

What to Do Now

Start by reviewing the table of contents. Depending on the type of retirement planning you have already started, you may want to go to a particular lesson. Otherwise, start with Lesson 1, "Planning for Retirement." By reading the entire book, you will understand what level of income you will need in order to retire; how much help you can expect from your employer; and most importantly, you will learn about investment strategies and tax strategies that will enable you to achieve your unique retirement goals.

PLANNING FOR RETIREMENT

In this lesson, you will learn how to establish basic retirement goals and learn how to create, implement, and monitor your retirement plan.

WHAT'S IN A RETIREMENT PLAN?

You need a road map for a retirement plan. A retirement plan should list your goals, your financial destination, and lay out a strategy to achieve those goals. Your retirement plan will show you how much you need to save each year to accomplish your goals.

Of course, your plan won't predict the future nor will it guarantee that you will reach your goals. It will also better prepare you for the decisions involved in making trade-offs that reach into the future.

THE PLANNING PROCESS

Retirement planning means organizing your approach to retirement. It is based on a thorough understanding of where you stand today, what your present financial condition is, and where you obtain your income and how you spend it. At the other end of the retirement plan is your retirement. How would you like to live after retirement and how much money will you need to accomplish that goal? The retirement plan will chart a course from the beginning to retirement (and beyond) showing you the tools you need to accomplish those goals. The plan will also help you cope with unexpected roadblocks that life may throw in your path as you save for retirement.

You should spend a great deal of time and effort in the retirement planning process. You may also have to spend money, especially if you seek the assistance of a professional financial planner.

tip   It may take hours to organize your financial records and to tabulate a personal cash flow statement to see how you currently use your financial resources.

CAN YOU AFFORD TO RETIRE?

As you begin to read this book, you will learn that few of us can afford to retire. Obviously, if retirement came tomorrow, there would be the safety net of Social Security. But few have built up enough in their employer's pension plan to afford retirement. And few of us would have enough savings to provide even the most basic standard of living.

In the lessons ahead, I'll show you that although you may possess more financial resources than you dared imagine, you are going to have to think long and hard about the sources you expect your retirement income to come from. Social Security is in financial trouble, many corporate pension plans are also in trouble. Now is the time to ask yourself some questions:

- What do you want when you reach the age at which you plan to retire?
- How much income will you need to live at the desired level during retirement?
- How will you reach those goals?

ASSESSING

The best way to assess your current resources is to prepare a personal financial summary, which should have two parts:

- A balance sheet
- A cash flow statement

The cash flow statement measures your cash inflow (income) and your cash outflow (expenses) over a period of time, usually a year. The difference between your income and your expenses represents your savings—the amount you will have to parley into the savings needed to finance your eventual retirement.

 Personal Balance Sheet. A balance sheet provides an accounting picture of what you own and what you owe. In other words, a personal balance sheet is a snapshot of your financial condition on a given day.

 Cash Flow Statement. A cash flow statement is a comparison of how money flows into and out of your life. It's a comparison of your income and expenses that should help you better understand how much money will be available for retirement planning.

IMPLEMENTING YOUR RETIREMENT PLAN

The money for your retirement will come from a variety of sources, which will be explained in later lessons. These sources include Social Security, employer-sponsored retirement plans, tax-free investments, and retirement-oriented investments and savings.

MONITOR YOUR RETIREMENT PLAN

Changes in your lifestyle, health, marital status, and the economy will all affect your retirement plan. At least once each year, after you receive year-end statements from your investment accounts, you should sit down on your own or with your financial planner and do the following:

- Update your personal financial summary, including your balance sheet and cash flow statements.
- Evaluate the performance of your investments for the past year.
- Evaluate and balance your investment portfolio if necessary to maintain the desired mix of investments.
- Ask the question: "Am I still on track to the retirement I want?"
- Ask "What has changed?" to see if any new developments in your life should prompt you to revise your goals.

SOURCES OF RETIREMENT INCOME

Retirement income comes in many forms. You will have some income that is paid monthly, such as Social Security and, perhaps, a pension. The rest of the retirement nest egg will probably be lump-sum amounts: your employee benefit plans, 401(k), profit-sharing, stock bonuses, and your personal investments (such as IRAs, mutual funds, stocks, and bonds) that are earmarked for retirement.

THE TIME VALUE OF MONEY

Retirement planning is a matter of setting goals, determining financial resources, and then taking the steps needed to reach those goals. A key element in that process is time. Understanding the relationship between time and money will help you develop the appropriate strategies for your retirement goals.

The more years that can be allowed to work for you, the more likely it is that you will be able to reach your retirement goals. Where money is concerned, time makes all the difference.

Time works its effect on money through a phenomenon known as compound interest.

Compound Interest. Compound interest means your money builds with interest as earnings from your deposited or invested money are reinvested and then generate earnings on their own. As if by magic, your money begets more money; it doubles, triples, quadruples, and so on as the years go by.

You can use the "Rule of 72" to understand the interplay of time and profit. When money doubles over a certain time, the end result of compounding periods and the rate of return per period will equal approximately 72. Therefore, if you pick an annual rate of return and divide it by 72, the answer will be a close approximation of the number of years required for your money to double. For example, at a seven percent return, your money doubles in roughly 10 years (72 divided by 7). At nine percent, it takes about eight years (72 divided by 9) for your money to double.

tip A dollar received today is worth more than a dollar received in the future. Why? Today's dollar can be invested and earn a return. A dollar in your possession today, for example, will be worth $1.23 three years down the road—assuming a seven percent annual investment return and no taxes or inflation.

In this lesson, you learned the importance of assessing your current resources, the value of creating a retirement plan, and that the key to retirement planning is to implement that retirement plan. In the next lesson, you will learn how to take stock of your personal financial resources.

THE STARTING LINE

In this lesson, you will learn how to assess your present financial resources, including your earnings, savings, employer-paid benefits, and Social Security benefits.

WHAT ARE YOUR RESOURCES FOR RETIREMENT?

The financial resources you will use in your retirement planning include such assets as your home, car, personal property, the money you have in the bank, and the value of your investments.

tip Don't forget that your financial resources also include protection you may have purchased in the form of life insurance or disability insurance policies. Most important, your financial resources include your earning power over the years ahead.

To maintain the same standard of living in retirement you enjoy today, you will need an annual retirement income of approximately 60 to 80 percent of pre-tax income or as much as 90 percent of your current earnings.

This table shows the percentage of different sources of income among those who have already retired:

Social Security	44 percent
Pensions and investments	43 percent
Employment	10 percent
Other	4 percent

Source: Employee Benefits Research Institute

TAKING A CLOSER LOOK AT YOUR FINANCIAL RESOURCES

There are a number of steps in the retirement planning process that will help you get a better handle on your current financial resources. Most important, you should set up a record keeping system.

Setting up a good record keeping system involves determining the amounts and sources of your income. Then you review your spending habits to determine where all of that income goes. Once these fundamental steps have been taken, establishing a system that will continually monitor that income and those expenses, a record keeping system, is a relatively simple matter.

Once established, a good record keeping system will allow you to prepare your financial statements, a statement of assets and liabilities, and a cash flow statement. The cash flow statement will help you create a useful budget.

FIGURING YOUR NET WORTH

Your net worth is the amount by which your assets (savings, investments, and property owned) exceed your liabilities (debt owed). Periodically determining your net worth helps you to gauge your financial progress toward your retirement goals.

If your income increases year after year, it may appear that you are getting somewhere. However, in all likelihood, your expenses will be increasing at the same time. Thus, the real measure of your monthly or year-to-year progress will be your net worth.

BUDGETING FOR RETIREMENT SAVINGS

A budget is an essential part of any successful retirement plan because it provides a moving picture of your financial situation. It can best be compared to the cash flow statement mentioned previously. The personal budget summarizes where your income comes from and shows how it is spent.

A budget shows what you spend for the essential items, such as food, clothing, and so on. The cash flow statement shows how you actually spend money during a given period.

> **!** Many of you will need almost $300,000 per year in future dollars in order to maintain a $60,000 lifestyle. That's right, four times what is needed today!

EMPLOYER PLANS

There are two basic types of plans: defined benefit and defined contribution. What do you know about your employer's plan? Whether your employer sponsors a defined benefit plan or a defined contribution plan, you are entitled to receive information about the plan.

Defined Benefit Plan. Promises to pay a specified amount to each person who retires after a set number of years of service.

Defined Contribution Plan. A defined contribution plan is a deferred retirement plan where benefits are based on the amounts contributed to each account. Often called "profit sharing" or "stock bonus plans," defined contribution plans are generally simple, more flexible, and less costly to administer than defined benefit plans.

Employer plans typically promise a retirement benefit or pension based on your salary prior to retirement and your total years of service. Under a defined benefit plan, the employer makes contributions to the plan to pay for the expected costs of the promised pension benefits.

Both employer and employee often contribute amounts to an employee's pension account and, upon retirement, the employee receives benefits based on what has been contributed. With a defined benefit plan, the employer promises a certain amount to the employee upon retirement and then contributes a varying amount until the account contains enough to pay that promised benefit.

A defined contribution plan is an "individual account" plan, which means that a separate account is established in your name to record the employer's contributions on your behalf and the associated investment gains and losses.

Unlike a defined benefit plan, a defined contribution plan does not promise or guarantee you a particular level of pension benefits at retirement. Rather, your financial benefits will depend on the total contributions made to the plan on your behalf and on the rate of return earned by those employer contributions.

DELVING INTO EMPLOYER-SPONSORED RETIREMENT PLANS

Exploring the fine print in the provisions of your employer-sponsored pension or benefits plan as a retirement resource should not be limited to any one area. For example, under most plans you are entitled to receive the following information:

- **Summary Plan Description.** This explains the fundamental features of your employer's plan, including eligibility requirements, contribution formulas, vesting schedule, benefit calculations, and even distribution options.

- **Individual Benefit Statement.** Although not required by law, it's common practice among employers and plan sponsors to send all participants periodic statements showing their current account balances or accrued benefits. If individual benefit statements are not automatically sent to you, you can request such a statement once each year from the plan's administrator. Here's what to ask for:

  - **Summary Annual Report.** This report describes the plan's aggregate financial status over the past year. This report is particularly meaningful if you participate in a defined benefit plan; it shows the overall funding status of the plan.

  - **Survivor Benefit Explanation.** This notice describes the survivor benefits available to spouses under certain types of pension plans.

The earnings portion of the preceding list will show a year-by-year record, going back to the start of your career, and lists your annual earnings up to the maximum taxable amount of Social Security ($61,200 in 1995). The statements may not include some or all of your earnings from the most recent year if Social Security has not yet had time to add them.

The benefit portion of the statement will give you an estimate of your future retirement, disability, and survivor benefits. Actual benefit amounts will depend on your age, your earnings history, and your expected future earnings.

You should submit a new Form SSA-7004 (Request for Earnings & Benefit Estimate Statement) every three years to check the accuracy of Social Security records regarding your employment. Check the figures carefully to see that you have been credited properly for each year you have worked. It will be much easier to correct errors if you file Form SSA-7004 periodically during your working years rather than waiting until you're ready to retire.

DISCOVER YOUR SOCIAL SECURITY BENEFITS

You can obtain an estimate of your Social Security retirement, disability, and survivor benefits by returning Form SSA-7004 to the Social Security Administration. Call 800-772-1213 for a form.

In this lesson, you learned to assess your personal resources, create your personal financial statements, and determine how much you can expect to receive under your employer-sponsored benefit plans and Social Security. In the next lesson, you will learn how to establish your retirement goals.

YOUR RETIREMENT GOALS

In this lesson, you will learn the importance of establishing goals for your retirement plan.

YOUR FINANCIAL OBJECTIVES OR TARGETS

While you may dream of retiring to live on a tropical island where beads are the only currency, in reality, you will have to give serious consideration to what your lifestyle will be like when you retire. The style of living you aim for and the living conditions you expect to experience after retirement will form the basis of your goals. Naturally, there are many factors that will affect even these rather basic goals.

- The time horizon, which is the period in which you will accumulate money for your goals

- The period of time in which accumulated retirement funds will be spent

DEVELOPING GOALS

You can begin developing your retirement goals by making a list of your goals. Review and refine this list as you formulate your investment strategies.

First, describe your goals in terms of quality rather than dollars and cents amounts. Then, begin to revise them. You might, for example, consider the basic questions in the following list. Your answers will form the basis for establishing your retirement goals.

Remember, there are no right or wrong answers to these questions. In fact, you'll probably constantly revise and change your answers as well as the financial course to your retirement goals that the list will help you establish.

- How much money will you really need to maintain the lifestyle you want and where will it come from?

- What can you do now to make sure you will have enough money?

- What will Social Security provide?

- How can you get started?

- Do you really want to quit work altogether? Can you afford to?

- What investment, tax savings, credit, and insurance strategies will help you put together the best worry-free retirement plan?

- How can you keep medical costs from wiping you out financially?

- When will it be financially feasible for you to retire?

Revising your retirement goals will make them increasingly specific and measurable. You should be able to revise each goal two or three times without stating it in terms of a particular dollar amount. Instead, express your goals as a percentage of your current income or current living expenses.

 tip Thinking of your goals in terms of today's dollars makes it easy to compare it to your present level of income and investments.

When looking at long-term spending needs, you can see an inordinate amount of concerns hedging on life expectancy and long-term planning. Some people feel that if they live beyond the age of 85, someone else's money will take care of them.

Effective planning of your retirement goals will help minimize the overconfidence that can occur when you expect someone else—whether it's the government, family members, or your company—to come up with the funds.

For every dollar you don't save for retirement by the age of 35, you will need to put aside almost four dollars at age 55 (assuming a seven percent rate of return in your investments).

Consider the questions in the following list (and remember to be realistic). Naturally, there will be some crystal-ball gazing, but you should consider realistic answers to these questions:

- When should you retire?
- How much will you spend during retirement?
- How will your spending change during retirement?
- How much should you adapt your current spending figures to reflect your post-retirement need?
- How long of a retirement should you plan for?

Now take a closer look at how to determine the answers to these all-important questions.

When Should You Retire?

The easy answer is when you're ready. In today's business climate, however, it isn't that simple. If you plan for an early retirement, you ensure that you can meet your retirement goals even if your job should be eliminated.

How Much Will You Spend During Retirement?

Although you may estimate what you will spend during retirement as a percentage of your current income, that figure can be refined quite easily.

What if you're 30 years or more from retirement? Who knows what your lifestyle will be like then. For all you know, inflation will make today's $1.50 loaf of bread cost $10.00.

Inflation

Although most economists feel that inflation will remain relatively low for the next 20 years (averaging four to six percent annually), don't think that a low rate won't affect you. Rising prices (and rising incomes) will affect your future spending needs and your future resources. If you don't take inflation into account, you'll be behind in reaching your retirement goals.

Let's say you have 12 years before you retire. If inflation averages four percent a year, you will need almost $100,000 in your first year of retirement to buy what $60,000 buys today.

Or, let's say you expect to receive a $30,000 per year pension over the course of a 20 year retirement period. If inflation averages just four percent, the buying power of that pension will be reduced to $13,700. In other words, if your pension is not independent of inflation (meaning that it increases as inflation does—and most aren't), you'll need to put away an additional $111,000 and invest it at seven percent merely to maintain the $30,000 buying power you started with.

TODAY'S LIFESTYLE

One easy way to do this is to plan for an average spending goal of 60 to 80 percent of your current spending and income during your retirement years and then refine it as you go along.

HOW WILL YOUR SPENDING CHANGE DURING RETIREMENT?

For most people, retirement consists of three phases: active, less active, and passive.

In the early years of your retirement, you are apt to be very active; you'll probably do a lot of traveling and entertaining. How about finally taking that trip to Europe you never got around to?

As the years go by, you'll probably become less active; your activities and lifestyle will change. Your spending will decline for entertainment as you cut back on that travel you did in the early years of retirement. Chances are, your medical bills will also begin inching up.

When you enter the passive years of retirement, you will probably see your spending increase again as medical and long-term care expenses increase (depending on your broad family plans and whether you have long-term care insurance). Naturally, your health, your spouse's health, and whether you have long-term medical care insurance will all become important factors during the passive years of retirement. Although I'll discuss long-term care along with other insurance options later, the importance of having insurance that will finance long-term nursing home or in-home care cannot be over-emphasized. Few retirees today have a family to take care of them or want to burden their families.

COPING WITH POST-RETIREMENT NEEDS

Not too surprisingly, when you establish your retirement goals you'll discover that you don't really have to make major adjustments in your present spending in order to meet your post-retirement needs.

Consider the differences between your spending today and your spending after retirement:

- You probably won't be commuting, so car expenses will decline.

- You will probably spend less on clothes.

- Personal loans or a home mortgage may be paid off by the time you reach retirement—and you may want to plan to save those no-longer necessary mortgage payments to add to your retirement nest egg.

- If you don't work during retirement, you won't pay any Social Security taxes.

- Because of lower income, income taxes should decrease.

- And, as mentioned, you may plan on an increase in travel and entertainment expenses.

Until you put pencil to paper and begin the actual retirement planning process, you can't reasonably understand what level of retirement income you may want or need.

How Long Will You Be Retired?

To be sure that you don't outlive your savings, plan for your retirement to last through the age of 90. If you have family members living well into their 90s, plan for an even longer retirement.

In this lesson, you learned the importance of establishing goals that incorporate factors such as when you expect to retire, how long you expect that retirement to last, and changes in your lifestyle and spending that must be considered when setting those goals. In the next lesson, you will learn how to evaluate the assets that will form the basis of your retirement.

4

ASSET EVALUATION

In this lesson, you will learn how to make the most of the assets you now have and about the amount of risk you must accept with your retirement investments to achieve the desired rate of return from those investments.

EVALUATING YOUR ASSETS

At this stage in the retirement planning process, you may not fully understand all about your assets and how valuable they are. But, you can still evaluate those assets with one eye on getting the most from them. Let's take a look at just one of those assets that you might understand a little about and see how you can utilize it in your retirement planning.

YOUR HOME

The equity in your home is not usually considered readily available until you reach the age of 55. That's the earliest age at which you can take advantage of a unique break in our tax laws (discussed in Lesson 8) that allows you to have up to $125,000 of profit tax-free. You can, of course, sell your home at any time and use the equity for your early retirement. However, if you do this before you reach age 55, you'll incur a substantial tax bill. That added price of not waiting until you are 55 means a sizable tax bill for any gains realized.

SELLING DOWN

Taking advantage of the unique tax breaks available to you as you near retirement, you can exploit the financial value of the equity in your home. The resulting tax savings can be used for investment purposes to speed up your retirement planning. Because of a one-time $125,000 capital gains tax exclusion available to those 55 or older, you may be able to trade down to a smaller home and thereby free a substantial amount of money from the proceeds of the sale. You can add those proceeds to your retirement investment portfolio.

> *tip*   The trading down strategy doesn't require that you move to a different part of the country. Moving to a less costly residence can make sense, even if you want to stay in the same area.

Generally, to be eligible, neither you nor your spouse can have used the exclusion before and the home must have been your principal residence for at least three of the five years before the sale date.

The tax rules allow you to take advantage of a onetime $125,000 exclusion on the sale of a home when you are over 55. If you choose not to take advantage of that unique tax break, you can defer taxes on any profit only by purchasing another home. That new home must have a value equal to or greater than the home you have sold in order for the gain to be deferred. Naturally, if or when you sell the new house and do not buy another replacement, you should be old enough to take advantage of the $125,000 exclusion or face a stiff tax bill on all of those profits deferred over the years.

There are a number of restrictions even with the basic deferral strategy. For example, you must buy and occupy the new residence within 24 months before or after selling your old home.

When you consider this unique tax break, you might want to consider whether you will have to move after retirement. After all, as you learned earlier with the three phases of retirement (active, not so active, and passive), you may prefer different types of residences.

For example, you may want to stay put during the active early years of retirement to continue your income-producing activities, and move to another location later. Or, you may plan to keep your present home until the later years of retirement, and then move to a retirement community that offers special-care facilities. Thus, if you will be selling your home at some later date to live with relatives or enter a retirement home, you should consider using the $125,000 exclusion later in your retirement.

REVERSE MORTGAGES

Reverse mortgage loans are a new form of mortgage. By taking out a reverse mortgage, you borrow against your property. Instead of receiving the proceeds in a lump-sum, they're paid to you in installments. You might be able to receive the proceeds in regular payments for a predetermined period of time (say 10 years), or the proceeds might be in the form of a credit line against which you can withdraw money when you want or need it. If you die or move from your house, of course, your reverse equity loan immediately becomes due.

Reverse Mortgage. This mortgage allows you to convert the equity in your home into installment payments that can provide you with monthly income for life.

Because there are no monthly payments due for a reverse mortgage, you don't need a salary or other earnings to qualify. The amount of monthly income you can obtain from a reverse mortgage depends on several factors, including your age, the prevailing interest rates, and the value of your property.

Usually, reverse mortgages are only available for borrowers age 62 or older. The older you are, the higher the reverse mortgage payments you receive will generally be because, presumably, you have less time to live. Reverse mortgages are an excellent way to benefit from the most common of assets.

Asset Allocation

A decision you have to make when evaluating your assets is the best way to use those assets and other assets acquired as part of your retirement plan. You need to evaluate those assets and the impact they will have on creating your retirement nest egg. How you apportion your money among cash, bonds, stocks, and hard assets will determine your investment return.

 Asset Allocation. Asset allocation is a method of targeting or choosing investments to achieve the highest possible return consistent with the degree of risk that you feel comfortable with.

Savings versus Investing

Although both words—saving and investing—cover the process of putting away money for retirement, there is a difference between saving for retirement and investing for retirement.

- Saving money means not spending it.

- Investing money means taking money you have already saved and doing something with it to earn a return. Investing usually involves risk.

RETURN

You probably have a good idea of what is meant by "return." It's the gain you make on an investment and your earnings. It's how much you are ahead. For example, if the principal or the amount invested is guaranteed not to vary, there's no gain or loss in value to add to the return equation.

When you purchase a corporate bond, for example, the return will have two elements: the amount of interest you receive plus or minus any gain or loss on that bond's price if it is sold before maturity.

RISK

Because you have a significant amount of time before you retire, you can accept a lower investment return and still achieve your retirement goals. High amounts of risk are not necessary because time will allow you to take the steps necessary to compensate in your ever-changing retirement plan or recoup any losses before retirement.

CAN FULLY INSURED SAVINGS BE RISK-FREE?

Bank accounts with balances less than the $100,000 Federal Deposit Insurance Corporation's (FDIC) insurance limit are free of one type of risk: the risk of loss of principal and interest. Those insured savings are vulnerable to purchasing power risk, or to the chance that money invested in them will have less purchasing power in the future than it does today.

> **tip** For every dollar you don't save for retirement by age 35, you'll need to put aside $4.00 at age 55 (assuming a seven percent rate of return on your investments).

SELF-DEFEATING RISK

Treasury bills and federally insured bank accounts are good examples of a hidden risk. Your principal and interest are both guaranteed by the government (up to insurance limits), but your return will most likely not keep pace with inflation. Between 1926 and 1994, for example, Treasury bills returned an average 3.7 percent annually, which barely beat the 3.1 percent inflation rate and lost on an after-tax basis. Only stocks returned a comfortable margin above inflation. Large company stocks beat the rate of inflation by more than seven percentage points, enough to pay taxes and still stay well ahead of rising prices. Small company stocks, which are considered to be among the riskiest of investments, beat inflation by more than nine percentage points.

UNHAPPY EVALUATIONS

Any investment purchased solely because of its level of risk, low or high, is likely to prove unsatisfactory. Similarly, any investment bought because of its level of return is also likely to be unsatisfactory. When selecting investments, you should look at both expected return and expected risk, then strike the appropriate balance for your particular retirement plan.

In this lesson, you learned the importance of evaluating your assets to help create a foundation for reaching your retirement goals. In the next lesson, you will learn how to chart a course to your retirement goals and to adjust the degree of risk to fit those goals.

GETTING THERE

In this lesson, you will learn how to begin to capitalize on your existing assets by beginning to build up your savings, and then moving into investing to reach your retirement goals.

THE IMPORTANCE OF SAVING

It isn't merely what you earn that will guarantee a comfortable retirement, but rather what you're able to save. Savings can come from diverting a portion of your income between now and retirement, from the return on your retirement savings and investments, or from evaluating your current spending habits.

The first step is to pinpoint where your money goes now. That means keeping records. Check stubs, receipts, and charge account statements admittedly provide the big picture. They document rent/mortgage, utilities, car payments, furniture, and other major purchases. However, the clues you now require are smaller:

- How do you spend your pocket money?

- How do you spend those $100 withdrawals from the ATM?

- What were those department store charges and credit charges for?

If you don't know the answers to these questions or if you aren't certain where all of your earnings go, perhaps a review of the previous lessons on the importance of budgets would be useful.

 tip One more monthly expense should, in reality, be retirement savings. You should shoot for 15 percent of your net income.

REFINANCE YOUR MORTGAGE WHEN RATES ARE LOW

An important part of answering the question of where all of your earnings go means taking a different view of your assets and savings with the idea of freeing up more money for retirement savings.

One way to do this is to refinance your mortgage. If the interest rate on your mortgage is relatively high, refinancing may lop $100 to $300 or more off your monthly payment. When you switch to a cheaper mortgage, don't let the savings slip away. Each time you write a check for your mortgage payment, write a second check for the money you saved and add it to your retirement nest egg.

TAP TAX BREAKS FOR SELF-EMPLOYED

If you're self-employed, consider arranging your business to take advantage of home-office tax deductions. Then put the money you save into your retirement plan. And, remember, you can be self-employed and work outside the home. This isn't always easy because the tax rules are pretty complex, as you'll learn in Lesson 8. However, a smaller tax bill thanks to a qualifying home office might mean more money available for retirement savings.

If you aren't self-employed, consider starting a for-profit business that will allow you to capture the same home-office tax deductions while creating extra income. Under income tax rules, employees may be entitled to an employee business expense deduction for using a home office. Again, the rules are complicated and not many employees can qualify. Converting a hobby into a business, on the other hand, often creates legitimate home office expense deductions, as well as deductions for other hobby-related expenses and even losses incurred (if you operate that activity as a business).

> *tip*   An added bonus to being self-employed is that you can open a Keogh retirement plan and make tax-deductible contributions of up to 20 percent of your self-employment income. You'll learn more about Keogh accounts in Lesson 9.

BE A SENSIBLE BORROWER

Not all debt is bad. The idea is to eliminate all unnecessary debt. Necessary debt can include a mortgage, car loans, and money borrowed to pay for education. These debts, managed properly, can be strategic financial moves aimed at helping you reach your retirement planning goals.

The other type of debt—the unnecessary, discretionary variety—tends to show up as escalating credit card balances, installment loans, and other revolving-credit type debt.

> **tip** Keep the cost of necessary debt as low as possible and keep discretionary debt to a minimum—zero is your goal.

BORROWING

Although you can still deduct your mortgage interest on your income tax return, tax deductions for interest on consumer or installment debt have been completely erased. Inflation is also extremely low, meaning that "expensive dollars" remain expensive. Also, credit card interest rates are extremely high especially when compared to what you can earn in a savings or money-market account.

Depending on your financial circumstances, eliminating all debt may not be possible or even desirable. Borrowing does have strategic advantages at times; you can use it as an asset to boost your wealth through leverage, to handle a financial emergency, or to speed up a necessary purchase. The all-important point is that you must manage credit wisely.

KEEPING DEBTS DOWN

How do you keep debts down?

- **Try to pay off your mortgage early.** There are no fancy formulas to doing this. Simply pay a little extra principal each month on your mortgage payment. Any amount—$25, $50, $100, or $200—will do. Essentially, each time you make a mortgage prepayment, you're investing the money at the same rate the mortgage company has been charging you. On a 10 percent mortgage, for example, the effect is like earning a risk-free, guaranteed 10 percent on your money. The savings generated by prepaying are dramatic.

Let's say you're 40 years old and just purchased a home with a 30-year, $100,000 mortgage at 10 percent interest. Your monthly payment is about $878, not including any payments for taxes or insurance.

By adding a measly $31 to your monthly mortgage payment, you can reduce the term of the mortgage by almost five years. The extra $9,300 you invest through those $31 monthly additions will knock a substantial amount off of what you would otherwise have to pay in interest over the life of the loan.

- **Save a bundle on credit card interest.** Among all types of consumer debt, credit card debt is the most expensive and the most damaging to any retirement plan. The real cost of large rising balances on credit cards is an eye-opener. If you're making the minimum two percent payment on a credit card that charges a $20 annual fee and 19.8 percent interest, it will take you 31 years and a total of $7,700 to pay off a $2,000 balance.

  If you have any money in a liquid account such as checking or savings, make paying off high-interest credit card debt your top priority. If your money is now earning five percent, for example, you can immediately boost your return to 18 percent by paying off a card balance that costs you 18 percent annually.

- **Tap the tax benefits of home-equity credit.** When borrowing is necessary, your plan should be to find the cheapest possible source of credit. For anyone who owns a home with enough built-in equity, the least expensive credit source is almost always a home equity loan or line of credit. The interest on these loans, up to $100,000, is deductible.

 Home Equity Credit. Home equity credit, in the form of either a fixed-term loan or a revolving line of credit, is when you borrow against the value of your home.

! Don't view home equity loans as a quick solution to your debt problems! Remember, if you can't repay these loans, you put your home at risk.

- **Stop taking out car loans.** A car loan is probably your second largest debt outside of a home mortgage. With auto loans being stretched to four or five years, by the time you pay it off, you're immediately ready to take out another car loan. Don't do it. Instead, free up some of that money to go into your retirement savings.

One way to break free is to use home equity credit to pay for your next car. Assuming a prime rate of seven percent, for example, you could buy your vehicle with an 8.5 percent home equity loan, making your after-tax cost just 6.12 percent (assuming you're in the 28 percent tax bracket). That might average about one-half of the cost of a regular, nondeductible car loan from the bank. Set your payments at a level that will retire the debt in no more than three years.

Chances are that you will still be driving your vehicle after the loan is paid. But don't stop making monthly payments. Steer that $300 to $400 into your nest egg account each month until it's time to buy another car.

TAX-DEFERRED SAVINGS

Tax-deferred savings are those savings and investments where taxes are postponed to a later date. In some cases, the taxes postponed will be income taxes postponed from when you earn the money and invest in the tax-deferred savings until you eventually withdraw it. Or, tax-deferred savings can merely grow, untaxed, until withdrawn. Tax-deferral can also mean investing money on which taxes have been deferred and watching it grow untaxed.

For most retirement savers, the benefits of tax-deferred savings far outweigh the lost flexibility and potential penalties. This is because you can build up your retirement assets in tax-deferred accounts much faster than you can with a savings account that isn't tax-favored. The best of all worlds is to save with pretax dollars (or get a current tax deduction for the money you put into the tax-deferred arrangement).

HOW MUCH FASTER CAN YOU ACCUMULATE MONEY?

Let's say that each year, for the next 25 years, you plan to contribute $8,000 of your earnings to a taxable investment that has an average annual return of eight percent. In reality, you only put away $5,520 because you have to pay income taxes on your earnings (31 percent of $8,000 is $2,480—the amount you pay in taxes). At the end of 25 years, after you pay your taxes each year, your investment will have grown to $269,793.

What if you set aside the same amount each year in a tax-favored, employer-sponsored 401(k) plan. While you'll explore the full advantages of 401(k) plans later in Lesson 10, for now you should know that money put into a 401(k) doesn't show up on your tax return and the earnings from those contributions continue to build up tax-free until you withdraw them.

What if your savings dollars earned the same return—eight percent—annually for 25 years? With your money in that 401(k), your earnings build up tax-deferred. You have the full $8,000 to put away because you can put the money into the plan before taxes. In 25 years, you would have an impressive $584,847 (or $315,054 more).

Naturally, tax-deferred isn't the same as tax-free. The dollars you put away are taxable when they're withdrawn—so you don't completely escape taxes. You simply postpone or defer them until you withdraw your money. Assuming that you withdraw your money in a single sum and pay taxes at 31 percent, you would still have $403,544, or $133,751 more than you would have had outside a tax-deferred savings plan.

In this lesson, you learned how you can set aside more money for retirement by cutting your debts and borrowing selectively. In the next lesson, you'll learn how to protect what you have, especially your power to earn money between now and your retirement.

PROTECTION

In this lesson, you will learn the importance of protecting your present assets and those assets that you will be acquiring between now and retirement.

LIFE INSURANCE

Obviously, the most important asset in your retirement plan is you. If your demise would result in economic hardship for your spouse or other loved ones, you're a candidate for life insurance.

But what kind of life insurance? And, how can you get that needed insurance without diverting any more than is absolutely necessary from your retirement savings?

> ***tip*** The payoff from life insurance, invested at a reasonable rate, should be enough for your family to carry on without you, after accounting for amounts available from Social Security and other assets you managed to accumulate.

The American Council of Life Insurance reports that the average insured household owns about $100,000 worth of insurance coverage.

THE INSURANCE CHOICES

Although there are many life insurance companies, each with a staggering array of products, there are really only two choices:

- **Term Life.** Life insurance, pure and simple, without any complicated investment or tax-deferred savings features.

- **Cash Value or Whole Life.** Life coverage that doubles as a retirement savings vehicle with the advantage of tax-deferred money growth over the long term.

You may already have trouble finding enough money to fund your 401(k) or IRA to the maximum each year. If this is the case, you should not shell out big money for cash value coverage laden with high up-front costs. It also makes little sense to shell out big money for an uncertain investment return, and a large "early surrender" penalty if you try to cash in the policy before 10 years or so.

If you have an existing whole-life policy that already has a built-up cash value, you would probably be wise to keep it. By now, that policy may be providing coverage at a very reasonable cost compared with what you would pay for a newly issued term policy.

TERM LIFE INSURANCE

Term life is the simplest, cheapest form of life insurance. It offers the most coverage for the lowest cost.

Term Life Insurance. Term life coverage is a specified amount of coverage that is paid to beneficiaries when the policyholder dies.

You select the level of coverage you want—$50,000, $500,000, or any amount—and pay an annual premium. If you die while you own the policy, your beneficiaries receive the money. The premium is based on the amount of coverage, your general health, and your age when you buy the policy. The premium rises as you grow older. A 40-year old, nonsmoker in good health, for example, can buy a $250,000 one-year policy for about $360 per year to start. At 50-years old, the same policy would cost about $808 per year.

With some policies, the premium rises each year; with others it's fixed for 5-, 10-, or 20-year periods. The 40-year old's premium under the policy just mentioned, for example, would be $400 for five years, $600 for the next five years, $920 for the next five years, and so on. Most plans are guaranteed renewable as long as you keep paying the premiums. To keep on track, be sure the policy you choose includes that renewal feature.

CASH VALUE INSURANCE

Term life insurance is an important component of most retirement plans. Cash value (whole life) insurance coverage can be a sound addition if the following applies to you and your unique situation:

- You need lots of insurance—more than $750,000, for example.

- You're already contributing the maximum to IRAs for you and your spouse, to a 401(k) plan if you qualify, or to any other tax-sheltered retirement savings plan available to you.

- You can afford it—which is to say that you're probably earning more than $150,000 per year.

- You plan to keep the insurance coverage for many years (10 or more).

If you meet these criteria, cash value coverage may be your best life insurance parachute. The main reason is that cash value life insurance doubles as a tax shelter for retirement savings. The shelter aspect works much the same as an IRA or 401(k): Cash inside the policy is granted the advantage of tax-deferred growth.

 Cash Value Insurance. Cash value or whole life insurance is a form of life insurance policy that offers protection in case the insured dies and also builds up a cash surrender value at a guaranteed rate that can be borrowed against.

A portion of what you pay in premiums each year goes to pay for the life insurance coverage, but the bulk of the money is devoted to the savings and investment features.

This type of policy has a value that increases over time and you can tap it for your retirement income. It's similar to a tax-favored savings plan with life insurance attached.

If you use cash value insurance as a tax shelter for retirement savings, there are two basic ways you can get your money out:

- **Borrowing.** You can borrow against the policy's cash value while keeping the insurance in force. Because it's a loan, the money is not taxed. Any loan

outstanding when you die is automatically deducted
from the proceeds of the policy.

- **Surrendering.** You can collect the entire cash
value by surrendering the policy and terminating
your insurance coverage. The payment is tax-free, up
to the amount you paid in premiums over the years.
Any excess is taxable.

Because commissions and fees take such a large bite out of
your cash value during the first few years, you need to keep
funding a policy for at least 10 years in order for your investment to pay off.

MEDICAL INSURANCE

Some type of medical or health insurance is a must. Don't
forget, however, that with the cost of health care so high—and
rising so rapidly—a lack of health coverage can jeopardize your
retirement—and your retirement plan—if you fall victim to a
severe illness or accident.

If you have employer-sponsored health coverage, either
through your company or your spouse's, make the most of it
now, before retirement, to free up resources for your retirement plan. Investigate the coverage you and your spouse have
now. You may be able to save thousands of dollars each year
by better managing your insurance benefits.

> **!** Don't assume that you can cancel a policy and
> immediately get new coverage. Before you cancel
> any insurance, however, find out the conditions
> under which you will be allowed to rejoin the group
> if your other coverage is ever in jeopardy.

PRIVATE DISABILITY INSURANCE

You probably don't want to hear about yet another retirement planning expense, especially if it relates to insurance. However, having disability insurance can give you peace of mind and relieve stress.

Long-term disability insurance protects you and your family against the loss of income due to a prolonged illness or crippling injury. Generally, the longer the term of disability, the greater the need for adequate coverage.

If you have assets—or future income—to protect, you can't afford to overlook disability insurance. First, review your employer's coverage to see what the policy covers. If your employer's policy is not sufficient, then you need to look into getting your own policy. And "sufficient" depends on your monthly living expenses (including savings for retirement).

Disability Insurance. Disability income policies are intended to replace a certain portion of your earnings when you can't work as a result of sickness or injury. In order to collect a benefit you must be disabled and also have suffered a loss of income.

Private disability insurance is designed to pay you a monthly benefit if you become disabled. You should shop for a private disability policy as carefully as you would look for a new car. Research thoroughly all policies you consider.

Disability insurance premiums are based on the amount of monthly benefit and a variety of other factors, including how soon benefit payments start after you become disabled, how long benefits will continue, and how disability is defined by the policy.

Medicare and Medigap Insurance in Your Future

When you reach the age of 65, Uncle Sam will step into the health insurance picture with Medicare, which will pay a portion of your health costs in retirement—but only a portion. You will also need Medigap coverage, which is paid for either by your former employer or by you, to cover what Medicare doesn't.

Medigap. Medigap insurance is private insurers' answer to bridging the gap between what the U.S. government's Medicare insurance system is willing to pay and what medical care actually costs. Usually you pay a premium, over and above Medicare, to a private insurance company for Medigap coverage.

Medicare. A Federal hospital insurance and supplementary medical insurance program for persons over the age of 65.

Medicaid. State and federal government public assistance programs that provide medical care for individuals whose incomes and total resources are below a certain level, without regard to their age.

Once fraught with confusion and fraud, Medigap insurance was radically revamped and a crop of new, simpler policies was introduced in 1992. Current annual premiums range from about $450 a year for a basic Medigap policy to $1,750 a year for top of the line coverage.

Your local Social Security office can provide a great deal of information including copies of the booklet "Guide To Health Insurance For People With Medicare." This free pamphlet describes the various types of supplemental insurance available.

LONG-TERM CARE INSURANCE

One of the major limitations of the Medicare program is that it excludes coverage for basic (or custodial) nursing home care, the cost of which now averages about $30,000 a year. To prepare for this potential liability, you can now buy long-term care insurance.

Long-Term Care Insurance. Long-term care insurance can be considered another form of disability insurance. However, instead of covering the loss of income from a disability, long-term care insurance protects against the costs associated with disabilities. The biggest of those costs is nursing home care.

Rather than reimbursing you for expenses actually incurred, these policies pay daily benefits ranging in amounts from $30 to $250. While premium rates vary depending on the level of benefits desired, such coverage will usually be more expensive if you wait until after retirement to sign up.

In this lesson, you learned the importance of protecting what you have and what you will acquire on the way toward your retirement goals. In the next lesson, you will learn who to contact to help plan your retirement.

7

GETTING THE HELP YOU NEED

In this lesson, you will learn about the type of professional assistance that is available as you plan for your retirement.

USING PROFESSIONAL ADVISERS

Finding a competent adviser is well worth the effort. There is no ideal way to locate those professionals, but word of mouth recommendations can be an important first step. There are many types of professional advisers. Some types of investments, such as stocks and bonds, can only be made through licensed brokers; certificates of deposit and savings accounts require the services and advice of a banker; insurance-related investments require insurance agents or brokers.

Some advisers and professionals come with the investment, such as professional money managers. Your only contact with a professional money manager may be through a mutual fund. Don't overlook managers who work with individual portfolios.

Professional Money Manager. A professional money manager is someone who manages money, either for a group of individuals or for a mutual fund. These managers usually have passed examinations to earn any one of several professional designations reviewed later in this lesson.

TAKING ADVANTAGE OF PROFESSIONAL MONEY MANAGERS

A professional money manager can custom-design an individual portfolio for each client. Your portfolio would reflect your specific investment goals and objectives. The services of professional money managers were once available only to very wealthy investors. Today, growing numbers of people can take advantage of these services because of the increasing number of advisers and many other factors that make their services less expensive to utilize.

Fees. Fees for professional money managers usually average from .75 percent to as high as 3 percent. (Comparatively, an average for stock mutual funds is a 1.5 percent management fee.) For their fees, professional money managers will custom-design an investment program based on your goals and risk parameters.

> ! If you place assets with a money manager, you must trust the manager's judgment. Most accounts are handled on a fully discretionary basis, meaning that the manager selects what to buy, when to buy it, and how much to buy.

WHAT ARE WRAP ACCOUNTS?

Since the mid-1980s, the brokerage industry has developed a service called the wrap account, which allows you to get professional money management services with as little as $100,000 in investable assets.

Wrap Account. A wrap account matches you with a professional money manager, who handles the actual investment of your money. The broker from whom you buy the wrap account is seldom the person who will actually manage your money.

Most wrap fees start at 3 percent (with the average being 2.3 percent). These fees are often negotiable.

> ! Wrap accounts seem like a great idea but can be controversial because the wrap fee is significantly larger than what you might pay to other money management services.

Overall, your decision to use wrap accounts comes down to a question of whether you want to pay a higher fee for personalized attention and professional money management. Naturally, professional money management services otherwise might not be available to someone with your account balance.

In April 1994, the Securities and Exchange Commission passed new rules governing the level of disclosure required of brokerage firms selling wrap accounts. Each firm is now required to disclose the following:

- Fee schedules, including what portion goes to the money manager and whether the fee is negotiable.

- How money managers are selected and reviewed, and the criteria used to judge performance.

- How performance numbers are calculated.

- Under what circumstances you will be allowed to contact the manager, such as whether you must call the broker first.

- The amount of information that the broker must give to the money manager about your investment goals and objectives, your risk tolerance, and so on.

USING FINANCIAL PLANNERS

A financial planner can be a valuable ally in reaching your retirement goals. You can link up with a planner on a continuing basis, or you can pay for advice periodically as a kind of second opinion on your plan.

 Financial Planner. A financial planner is someone you consult about your money. The planner may or may not have professional qualifications. The planner may simply offer suggestions about your savings and investments, or the planner may actually manage a portfolio for you.

A good financial planner will see to it that your investments are diversified and consistent with your retirement goals. A good financial planner will also help you anticipate the tax consequences of any financial decision that might affect your retirement nest egg.

tip Many financial planners are registered with the Securities and Exchange Commission (SEC) as investment advisers. This means that they can serve as money managers for their clients, creating and managing investment portfolios and charging a fee comparable to that charged by mutual funds. (Mutual funds are discussed in depth in Lesson 11.)

Ideally, you should look for a financial planner who has received some training in the field and also has experience. There are three certificates that financial planners can have:

- **Accredited Personal Financial Specialist (APFS).** This certification is conferred by the American Institute of Certified Public Accountants (AICPA) and can be held only by CPAs. The majority of those with the APFS designation operate on a "fee only" basis, which you'll learn about later in this lesson.

- **Certified Financial Planner (CFP).** The CFP designation is granted to individuals who have completed an intense study program, passed a comprehensive examination, and have fulfilled an experience requirement.

- **Chartered Financial Consultant (ChFC).** This certification is awarded by the Bryn Mawr, Pennsylvania-based American Society of Chartered

Life Underwriters (CLU) and Chartered Financial Consultants (ChFC) to individuals who complete a 10-section course of study and who pass two examinations.

 Registered Investment Advisers. These individuals are registered with the Securities and Exchange Commission. By law, people who give investment advice must be registered.

Other professionals—such as bankers, insurance agents, or brokers and stockbrokers—who practice in specialty areas of retirement planning may also be able to assist you in attaining specific goals.

How Financial Planners Are Paid

Financial planners are compensated for their efforts on your behalf through fees, commissions, or a combination of the two.

A fee-only planner is paid on an hourly basis or a retainer basis. If a fee-only planner spends 10 hours devising an investment strategy for you, you are billed for 10 hours work at an hourly fee. Alternatively, the planner may arrange a fixed fee.

A commissioned planner earns his or her income by commissions charged as part of the cost of investments and insurance products that you buy through the planner.

Some planners combine these two sources of compensation, earning income through both fees and commissions. Fees are earned by providing a review of your financial situation together with specific recommendations. If you decide to accept those recommendations, the planner will earn commission on the investment and insurance products that you purchase while implementing their recommendations.

Don't Forget the CPAs

Certified Public Accountants (CPAs) practice in every town in the country. A CPA provides a variety of services and most are well-qualified to advise you on tax matters and/or to prepare your income taxes.

Many CPAs have also become proficient (and even certified) in personal financial planning. The APFS degree designates a CPA who is qualified to help you with your personal financial planning needs.

When Do You Need an Attorney?

A family attorney is essential for preparing necessary estate planning documents, such as your power of attorney and will.

You may outgrow your attorney's expertise if your investments and assets grow to a level that will require more sophisticated planning techniques.

In this lesson, you learned about the many professionals who can help you plan and implement your retirement plans. In the next lesson, you will learn about the income tax rules that affect your retirement planning.

Using Tax Rules as a Planning Tool

In this lesson, you will learn how to cut your taxes and take advantage of tax strategies as you plan for your retirement.

Don't Pay More Taxes than You Have To

Surprisingly, despite tax laws that defend the right of every individual to pay only minimum permissible taxes, many people pay more taxes than they have to.

Tax planning is a crucial part of retirement planning for those who are under 40. But it's just one part. Even though any investment or financial decision should include an evaluation of its tax ramifications, no transaction should be made solely or even primarily on that basis alone.

Using Tax Deferral to Increase Savings

Taxes work as a drag on the power of compounding by substantially reducing your effective rate of return. If you're in the 28 percent tax bracket, you keep only 72 percent of all dividend or interest earnings that are exposed to taxes. In the 36 percent bracket, you retain only 64 percent of pretax earnings. And in the top 39.6 percent bracket, you keep just 60.4 percent.

The best outcome where taxes are concerned, obviously, is not to have to pay them. That's a major reason why so many investors favor municipal bonds. Interest on municipal bonds is not generally subject to federal income taxes (although state or local income taxes may be due if you own municipal bonds issued outside of your home state).

The next-best tax strategy is to delay or defer paying taxes as long as possible. The longer you can keep your money from being taxed and leave all of your earnings free to compound, the easier it will be for you to reach your retirement goals.

Investments not protected in tax-deferred assets are fully exposed to the eroding effects that rising tax rates have on long-term compounding. As a result, it usually makes sense to direct as much savings as allowed to retirement accounts that offer shelter for pretax contributions, such as a 401(k) plan.

Other savings vehicles, such as annuities (where you can obtain tax deferral on earnings but no up-front tax deduction on your contributions), may also make sense for you. Keep in mind, however, that higher costs and certain restrictions typically associated with annuities may offset some of the benefits of tax deferral.

Annuities. An annuity is a tax-sheltered investment, usually sponsored by an insurance company, that pays a death benefit and provides a return on your premium.

Naturally, when you take money out of a tax-deferred account, taxes will be due on your withdrawal. Remember, however, that the purpose of investing long term is to generate money for your retirement.

> **tip** If tax deferral will enable you to accumulate a substantially larger amount of capital for retirement, compared to what you could accumulate on a fully taxable basis, you will be better off.

Tax Exempt Investments

Why invest in tax-free securities and tax-free mutual funds? With few exceptions, interest earned from municipal investments is exempt from all federal income taxes and, in many instances, from state and local taxes.

> **tip** Here's a general rule of thumb: consider investing in tax-free securities if your taxable income is expected to place you in the 28 percent federal tax bracket or higher.

The Importance of Capital Gains

A good, sound retirement plan for anyone under the age of 40 requires dealing with the capital gains tax effectively. In spite of the tax legislation (real and proposed) in recent years, capital gains remain an important element in your retirement planning.

Capital Gains. Capital gains refers to the tax due when a stock or other capital asset is sold at a price that is higher than when it was purchased.

When stock or property is sold at a gain, the amount of the gain is subject to federal income tax at capital gains tax rates. Thus, when you sell your home or even stocks, bonds, and other investments, the profit or gain will usually be taxed at the special capital gains rates. This means that while the profit may be enough to put you into the top tax bracket, the highest bracket you will pay taxes on for those capital gains is presently 28 percent.

UNREALIZED CAPITAL GAINS

Unrealized capital gains—gains on stock and property that you hold—are not subject to income taxes. This is a major tax advantage and many investors have accumulated considerable wealth by buying and holding stocks and property. The value of these stocks and property rises over the years and yet there is no tax bill to pay.

Because unrealized gains are not taxed, you have complete control over the timing of when you will pay your taxes on those capital gains.

REALIZED CAPITAL LOSSES

Not all stock investments are winners. Inevitably, some will have to be sold at a loss. Fortunately, realized capital losses can be used to offset realized capital gains—often a smart move.

In addition to offsetting capital gains, up to $3,000 of excess capital losses may be utilized each year to offset other taxable income.

The ever-changing tax rules allow you to utilize those losses you may incur to offset gains within the same category or class. However, only $3,000 of losses may be claimed on the income tax return each year.

TAX BREAKS FOR SELLING YOUR HOME

Although you may have a long time until retirement, you will probably move and sell your home several times between now and that date. As retirement approaches, you may want to utilize the equity accumulated in that home to increase your retirement savings or to buy a smaller, mortgage-free home. You cannot accomplish that if taxes have taken large bites out of that home equity.

When it comes to selling your principal residence, tax laws offer two significant tax breaks to homeowners. The first is a one-time exclusion of up to $125,000 in capital gains on the sale of a primary residence. You are probably more familiar with the second tax break: you can defer the taxes on your home-related capital gains by purchasing a more expensive residence. Used together, these tax breaks can allow you to trade down (buy a less expensive home), pay less tax on the gain, and free up cash for your retirement.

TRADING DOWN AFTER 55

Using the once-in-a-lifetime exclusion is a key question for anyone wanting to fund a portion of their retirement income needs with their home equity. If you are age 55 or older on the date of sale, you can use the once-in-a-lifetime exclusion rule to sell your primary residence and exclude up to $125,000 of profits from taxation. Any amount in excess of $125,000 is taxed as a capital gain.

tip   You can make a really impressive tax-free maneuver by using both the $125,000 exclusion and the rollover-of-gain break. By combining these two provisions, you may collect more than $125,000 in profit and buy a home that costs as much as $125,000 less without paying a single penny in taxes.

If you paid $145,000 for your house in 1974, and 20 years later pay off the mortgage and sell it for $380,000 plus $20,000 in selling costs, you collect $215,000 profit. Because you are 56 years old, you sensibly opt to take the one-time exclusion so $125,000 of your $215,000 gain would be tax free to you—forever.

Now you want to purchase a new home. You may think you have to find one of equal value to your old one so you'll qualify for the rollover-of-gain break. However, when figuring how much you must spend on a new home, the rules allow you to subtract the amount of your exclusion ($125,000 from the selling price of your old house, which was $380,000). So you must spend only $255,000 for a new house—not $380,000.

As long as your new principal residence costs $255,000 or more, you defer paying taxes on your remaining gain of $90,000. You also reduce the basis or book value of your new home by only the $90,000 gain that you don't pay taxes on now. The $125,000 is excluded from taxes.

> *tip*
> When borrowing is necessary, you should try to find the cheapest possible source of credit. For anyone who owns a home with enough built-up equity, the least expensive credit source is usually a home equity loan or line of credit.

TAX PLANNING AS PART OF RETIREMENT PLANNING

Tax planning consists of much more than simply taking advantage of every possible deduction or utilizing tax deferred savings. It consists of developing a coherent, long-term strategy to reduce your taxes over the coming years. Tax planning is a year-round process, not just something to do during the month of December.

> **!**
> One of the most common tax planning mistakes you can make is to become "tax driven" rather than "tax aware." Tax driven is when you want to reduce taxes at any cost. Tax aware is when you're knowledgeable about the tax ramifications of a particular action.

In this lesson, you learned how to use tax rules to help you legally defer or delay paying taxes on your savings, thereby making larger amounts available for investing or saving. In the next lesson, you will learn about the tools that you may already possess that will give you a tremendous step toward your retirement goals—if you take full advantage of them.

THE FOUNDATION OF YOUR RETIREMENT PLAN

In this lesson, you will learn about the basic tools of retirement planning, including your investments and your employer benefits.

PENSION PLANS

A pension plan from a current or previous employer is one of the most important tools in your retirement planning arsenal. The more generous the plan and the more effectively you tap its benefits, the more easily you can attain your retirement goals. And, with nearly half of the workforce made up of two-earner couples, a record number of future retired couples will enjoy a double dose of potential pension income.

Every employer puts a different spin on its retirement benefits package. If you participate in several employers' plans over the course of your career, you may be entitled to collect from more than one plan.

How Does Your Employer's Plan Work?

Sizing up your own pension plan at work will give you the tools needed to fit this important piece into your overall retirement plan.

More than 80 percent of large employers have a two-part plan. Part one, a traditional benefit plan paid for by the company, is considered the pension cornerstone. Part two, the self-directed portion, allows employees to boost retirement benefits through their own savings, which are often magnified by matching contributions from the employer.

Traditional Pension Plan. A traditional pension plan is one in which your employer sets aside a specific amount of money that you will get when you retire. Generally, you don't have to contribute to this plan although in many cases you can add to it if you want.

Self-Directed Pension Plans

There has been a dramatic shift away from traditional pension plans, in which employers assume all responsibility for making contributions and managing the money, and toward self-directed plans that force you into an active role on both counts. About 40 million Americans are covered by self-directed plans.

In taking an active role in any pension plan, you have the option of deciding what types of investments those pension funds should be invested in. You may have the opportunity to direct the funds earmarked for your retirement to be invested in government bonds or, perhaps, stocks and bonds may be more appropriate for your unique retirement plan.

Defined Benefit Plans. Defined benefit plans, also known as self-directed pension plans, operate with both you and your employer putting money into an account with your name on it. As employee, you make the decisions about how this money is invested. If you leave your job, for retirement or other reasons, you can probably take the money with you.

These plans guarantee to pay you a specified amount when you retire, based on your salary, age, and years of service—in other words a defined or specific benefit. They are backed by a government insurance agency called the Pension Benefit Guarantee Corporation (PBGC).

Most plans are designed so that the pension benefit plus Social Security benefits will replace 60 to 70 percent of an employee's preretirement income. This is a good deal, when you consider that most retirement goals call for replacing 80 percent of that income. Remember, though, that one problem with defined benefit plans is that many are not indexed for inflation; so, as 10 to 20 years go by, inflation may have actually reduced the percentage contributed to these plans. Social Security is, of course, indexed for inflation.

To receive the maximum pension, most defined benefit plans require that you work at the company for 30 years and wait until "full retirement age." That's usually 62 or 65, but some companies use a point system that allows you to retire with full benefits once your age plus years of service equal a certain number of points.

ARE YOU AN ACTIVE PARTICIPANT?

Look at your W-2 form. It includes a Pension Plan check box; this can only be checked by your employer. If the box is checked, you're an active participant in your employer's pension plan. If it isn't checked, you should know the active participation rules.

The IRS says that it makes no difference whether you actively participate in a defined benefit plan. It matters only that you're eligible to participate. Unfortunately, the rules are different for a defined contribution plan. Here you are considered an active participant if, during the year, you contribute money or your company contributes money on your behalf.

Remember, however, you are not an active participant if the only money that's added on your behalf during the year is earnings from the investments already in that plan.

GOVERNMENT PROTECTION

In a defined benefit plan, the employer is legally committed to make sure there's enough money in the plan to pay the guaranteed benefits. If the company fails to meet that obligation, the federal government will step in to reimburse the plan's participants.

Defined benefit plans are the only type of pension insured by the Pension Benefit Guarantee Corporation (PBGC). The insurance works in much the same way that the Federal Deposit Insurance Corporation backs up your bank account.

If your plan is covered (most are) and the sponsoring company goes under, PBGC will take over benefit payments, but only up to a maximum (about $31,000 a year in 1995) payment adjusted periodically for inflation.

Individual Retirement Accounts (IRAs)

For those who have no way of participating in 401(k) plans or other self-directed, tax-deferred retirement plans (or if you have maximized your 401(k) savings), the next best place for your money may be an individual retirement account (IRA). IRAs may have lost some of their luster, but they can still be a key ingredient in your retirement plan.

 Individual Retirement Account. IRAs are investment vehicles specially intended to let you set aside money on a tax-deferred basis.

An IRA's appeal used to be that, as long as you were not older than 70 and a half, the contributions you made to an IRA were fully tax deductible. Today, however, that's true only for people whose incomes are below specified levels or who aren't eligible to participate in an employer-sponsored retirement plan.

Under current tax laws, if neither you nor your spouse participates in an employer-sponsored retirement plan (that is, are active participants), you may contribute and deduct on your income tax return up to $2,000 for yourself and $2,000 for your spouse. If your spouse is not employed, then his or her contribution is reduced to $250.

If you or your spouse actively participates in an employer-sponsored retirement plan, another set of rules applies:

- The IRS says that if you're single and are an active participant, you may deduct your full contribution only if your adjusted gross income (AGI) is $25,000 or less. Your allowable deduction drops $10 for each

$50 you earn above $25,000 until you reach $35,000, when the deduction phases out entirely.

- If you're married and file jointly, and if either one of you is an active participant, you get a full deduction only if your AGI is $40,000 or less. Your deduction drops by $10 for each $50 in income up to $50,000, where the deduction vanishes.

- Filing separately won't help. If married couples file separately, no tax deduction is allowable to either person.

HOW MANY IRAS CAN YOU HAVE?

The IRS doesn't care if you set up one IRA or a dozen. You may set them up at as many financial institutions as you want. However, be careful when you open multiple accounts. Most institutions charge you annual fees, up to $50 or more, to maintain your IRA. So, if you maintain many small accounts and they all charge fees, your investment return effectively drops.

tip

You're allowed to deduct the annual maintenance fee as a miscellaneous itemized deduction. But you may write it off only if the following are true:

- If you pay it out of separate funds

- If it and all other miscellaneous itemized deductions exceed two percent of your adjusted gross income

IRA Investing

The trustee of your IRA may be the institution or institutions where you maintain your IRA, such as a bank, savings and loan, mutual fund, and so on. You can manage your account yourself, if you want, investing as you see fit. If that's your choice, you would use a bank or brokerage house as custodian of your IRA. You can invest your IRA in most regular investment vehicles, such as certificates of deposit, mutual funds, and stocks or bonds.

However, you don't have total freedom when it comes to investing your IRA dollars. You can't buy a life insurance contract, although annuities are allowed. Art objects, antiques, gold or silver coins (except gold and silver coins minted by the U.S.), stamps, and other collectibles are also not permitted as IRA investments.

If you do use IRA dollars for prohibited investments, Uncle Sam treats the current year investment as a withdrawal from your account. That means you must pay tax on that amount at ordinary tax rates and if you invest in the item before age 59 and a half, you must pay an additional 10 percent penalty.

There's one more investment you should avoid when it comes to your IRA: municipal bonds or other tax-free investments. As you know, the money in your IRA account is taxed when you withdraw it. Municipal bonds are tax-free. So, by putting those bonds in your IRA, you're converting tax-free income into taxable income.

Creating Your Own Benefit Plan: The Keogh

The basic retirement program for self-employed individuals is called a Keogh plan, named after Daniel Keogh, the

Congressman whose legislation authorized the tax break that makes the plan so popular.

 Keogh Plan. A Keogh plan is a retirement plan for self-employed people that lets you set aside a certain percentage of your income on a tax-deferred basis.

Under a Keogh plan, contributions are fully tax deductible. The plan also serves as a tax shelter—there's no tax on earnings until you withdraw the money, presumably in retirement. Contributions to your personal pension plan are always fully tax deductible, no matter how high your income and regardless of whether you or your spouse is covered by another retirement plan. There's no such thing as a nondeductible contribution as there is with an IRA.

In fact, you can have an IRA in addition to your Keogh. Of course, whether IRA contributions would be deductible depends on your income, because a Keogh is considered an employer-sponsored plan for purposes of IRA deductibility tests.

How much can you contribute? That depends on how much self-employment income you have and what kind of Keogh you choose. The limits generally range from 15 percent to 25 percent of your self-employment earnings to a maximum of $22,500 to $30,000 per year.

The major drawback to having your own small business pension plan is this: if you have employees, they must be included in the plan and you must contribute the same percentage of income to their accounts as you contribute to your own.

MORE SELF-CREATED RETIREMENT BENEFIT PLANS: SEPs

There is an alternative to the Keogh. The SEP (also known as a business IRA) permits a fully tax-deductible contribution far above the $2,000 limit for individual IRAs.

 Simplified Employee Pension. A SEP is easy to set up and requires far less paperwork than a Keogh or other small business pension plan. SEPs deliver important tax savings to both employers and employees.

Your business or self-employment taxable income is reduced by the amount of money that you put into your SEP. The money in your plan, including earnings on investments, grows untouched until you withdraw it.

Anyone with income from self-employment is eligible to open a SEP: sole proprietors, partners, owners of corporations or S corporations, even freelancers and moonlighters.

A SEP is a cross between a profit-sharing Keogh plan and an IRA. Your contributions go into a special SEP-IRA. You can contribute as much as 15 percent of your net self-employment earnings, up to a maximum of $22,500.

In this lesson, you learned the importance of contributing to a tax-deferred account to build your retirement portfolio. In the next lesson, you will learn more about the many ways your employer can help you provide for your retirement.

BUILD YOUR RETIREMENT FUNDS ON COMPANY TIME

In this lesson, you will learn how to take full advantage of your employer benefit plans to reach your financial goals.

PROFIT-SHARING PLANS

One of the best ways to help build your retirement savings is to use your employer's profit-sharing plan.

Profit-Sharing Plan. Allows workers to share in company profits, usually based on a percentage of their salary.

It used to be that a company could make contributions to this type of plan only if it posted a profit. However, under current laws, a company may make contributions to a profit-sharing plan even if it reports no earnings. Also, it may change the amount of contributions from one year to the next.

Normally, profit-sharing contributions are allocated to employee accounts in proportion to their current salary. The company—not you—decides how the money in the plan is invested.

Profit-sharing plans have a number of benefits. If the company does well, the profit-sharing arrangement lets you participate in that success. A company that grows wildly could net you a sizable retirement nest egg. If a portion of the money in this plan is invested in stocks, you have another important tool for beating inflation.

A drawback is that the ultimate size of your nest egg is not entirely predictable because the size of the contributions can vary drastically from year to year.

Employee Savings Plans

Another popular employer benefit is a savings plan. The most common type of savings plan is the 401(k) plan.

401(k) Plan. A 401(k) plan is an employer savings plan that lets you set aside a percentage of your salary in a tax-deferred account. A 401(k) plan, like an IRA and a deferred annuity, is a tax-deferred savings plan. You pay no federal or state (except in Pennsylvania) income taxes on the dollars you contribute until you withdraw them, usually at retirement. Your interest, dividends, and other earnings from that plan accumulate tax-deferred until you take them out. The real advantage of the plan is that many employers match your contribution, usually by 50 percent.

If you participate in your employer's 401(k) plan, you can currently defer up to $9,240 in earnings each year. That amount is indexed to inflation but is adjusted upward only when the cumulative growth in the consumer price index is large enough to cause the deferred limit to increase by $500. The actual annual limit on deferrals may be lower than the legal limit for some plans or some employees. Many employers will match some or all of your contribution up to a certain limit, for example, six percent of your salary.

REASONS TO USE 401(K) PLANS

There are many reasons why you should participate in a 401(k) plan:

- To reduce your current tax bill and accumulate retirement savings on a tax-deferred basis

- The "forced savings" aspect—you pay yourself first and never see the money.

- To get an automatic return on your money—often as much as a 50 percent contribution from matching contributions by your employer (depending on the type of plan).

- To collect the matching contributions from the company, and additional earnings.

EMPLOYER CONTRIBUTIONS

You may not own matched funds immediately because that portion of the contribution is usually subject to a vesting schedule. With a vesting schedule, the employee takes ownership of the contribution over a period of time. The period of time is usually based on your length of service, but it cannot be longer than seven years (five years is the standard).

401(K) LIMITS

Not too surprisingly, there are limits on the amount you can contribute to a 401(k) plan. The IRS sets several ceilings on 401(k) contributions. The following are the most important:

- You may put aside a percentage of your wages (the percentage allowed depends on your company's plan) as a pretax contribution into a 401(k) plan, but this contribution cannot be more than $9,240 (as of 1995). Many employers also allow 401(k) contributions to be taken out of bonuses.

- The maximum salary that can be used to figure your contribution to a 401(k) plan is $150,000. This amount is adjusted annually for inflation.

401(K) INVESTMENT OPTIONS

When you're in a 401(k) plan, you must learn how to manage the account; you must make all of the investment decisions. You're restricted only by the investment options that your company makes available to you.

These investments often include equity mutual funds, shares of stock in your company, money market accounts, guaranteed investment contracts (GICs), and government securities (such as Treasury bills) all of which will be discussed in Lesson 11.

tip By law, a 401(k) plan must allow you to choose from at least three investment options. Also, under recently issued U.S. Department of Labor rules, companies will be able to minimize their exposure to investment-related claims by providing you with detailed information so you understand the choices available to you and the risk associated with each option.

ADDITIONAL BENEFITS FROM A 401(K)

After taking full advantage of the 401(k) plan offered by your employer, the next step is to make after-tax contributions to your 401(k).

Not all plans allow after-tax contributions, but if yours does, it's similar to making a nondeductible IRA contribution without the $2,000 limitation. Your after-tax contributions will, however, be limited by the percent limits on your 401(k) plan.

NONPROFIT EMPLOYEE SAVINGS PLANS

If you work for a nonprofit organization, such as a hospital, university, or public school, you are eligible for a 403(b) plan, which is similar to the 401(k) plans of private industry. Your employer may sponsor a 403(b) or, if not, you may be able to arrange for an individual 403(b) plan through an insurance company or mutual fund. As with a 401(k) plan, your salary is reduced by the amount of your contribution to a 403(b) plan. The annual contribution limit is 25 percent of your salary, with a limit of $9,500. That limit will be adjusted upward for inflation when the 401(k) ceiling ($9,240 as of 1995) catches up with it.

> **tip**   For most retirement savers, the benefits of tax-deferred savings far outweigh the lost flexibility and possible penalties. This is because you can build up your retirement assets in tax-deferred accounts much faster than you could with a savings account that is not tax-favored.

There's also a section 457 plan aimed at the need for retirement benefits for employees of colleges, universities, and local government entities.

DO SAVINGS PLANS PAY?

Let's say you're a taxpayer in the 31-percent tax bracket. Each year for the next 25 years, you plan to contribute $8,000 of your earnings in a taxable investment with an average annual return of eight percent. First, that $8,000 is only $5,520 after you pay taxes. At the end of 25 years—after you pay your taxes each year—your investment will have grown to $269,793.

But let's say you set aside the same amount in your employer-sponsored 401(k) plan, and contributions earned the same eight percent return annually for 25 years. With your money in a 401(k), the earnings build up, tax-deferred. Also, you have the full $8,000 to put away because you can put the money in the plan before you pay taxes. In 25 years, you could have an impressive $541,412 (or $271,619 more).

Making the Most of the Benefits

Obviously, tax-deferred isn't the same as tax-free. The money you put away is taxable when you withdraw it, so you won't escape taxes entirely. You simply postpone them until you withdraw your money.

Using the examples in the previous section, if you withdraw your money in a single sum and pay taxes at 31 percent, you would still have $373,574—that's $101,955 more than you would have outside a tax-deferred savings plan. You would probably put the money into a rollover IRA at retirement, take money out as you need it, and thus pay taxes only on the money you withdraw at the time you withdraw it. This way, the remaining balance would continue to grow tax-deferred, making the argument for the tax-deferred savings even stronger.

If you and your spouse can contribute in pretax dollars and allow those dollars to grow tax-deferred, you have the best of all worlds. Even if you can only use tax deferral on the earnings, you're still likely to build your retirement nest egg faster.

Employee Thrift and Savings Plans

Employee thrift and savings plans usually require after-tax contributions that are either wholly or partially matched by the employer's contributions. Even though there are no immediate tax benefits, you get something for nothing (your employer's contribution) and your savings will benefit from accumulating tax deferred.

EMPLOYEE STOCK OWNERSHIP PLANS

Employee stock ownership plans (ESOPs), are one type of profit-sharing arrangement.

This is a way to acquire stock in the firm you work for at little or no commission cost or even at a share-price discount. You'll pay taxes on the value of the shares only when you take possession or leave the company. In the meantime, the stock can appreciate tax-free as a part of your retirement nest egg. Even if you leave the company and take the stock with you, you can roll it over into an IRA.

To determine whether an ESOP fits into your retirement plan, take a look at any other retirement benefits your company offers. An ESOP is an investment in the company that you work for—not a traditional pension plan.

IRAS AND ANNUITIES

The next step when evaluating the benefits offered by your employer is to consider an IRA. Even though you might not be able to get a tax deduction for the annual contribution, the earnings grow tax-deferred.

Another tax-deferred option that plays a role in maximizing the contributions of your employer is annuities. With annuities, you can invest your money and let it grow while keeping the IRS away from the earnings as long as possible.

In this lesson, you learned how to take advantage of employer savings and retirement plans. In the next lesson, you will learn what other investments you should consider.

INVESTING CASH RESERVES

In this lesson, you will learn about cash and "cash equivalent" investments that play a major role in retirement planning. Cash equivalent investments are those investments that can be readily converted into cash, such as CDs, money market funds, Treasury bills, and the like.

REDUCING RISK IN YOUR PORTFOLIO

You invest in cash equivalent investments and bonds to provide a stable level of income and to reduce overall portfolio risk.

Cash Equivalent Investments. Cash equivalent investments are issued by borrowers, such as government agencies, large corporations, and banks, with strong financial positions. There is little, if any, credit risk and the short maturities of this type of investment protect against significant loss of principal should interest rates change.

Naturally, if interest rates plunge, the return on your cash investments can drop to very low levels because interest income is the only type of income (little gain or appreciation) received from this type of investment.

Interest. Interest is the cost of using someone else's money. It is also income derived from a bank account or investment.

tip
You pay a price for safety and liquidity in the form of lower yields. Historically, cash and cash equivalent investments have provided yields that have barely exceeded the annual rate of inflation. Inflation, after all, is the main enemy to combat for anyone under the age of 40.

The primary reasons you would consider investing in cash equivalents is to maintain a reserve for emergencies, and as a short-term, low-risk place to put funds awaiting investment in other vehicles.

SAVINGS BASICS

With savings, you put an amount of money in a savings account or in a cash equivalent, such as money market accounts, Treasury bills, or certificates of deposit (CDs). The amount saved usually earns interest. At the end of the period, you withdraw the funds originally deposited along with any interest the funds earned while you entrusted them to the bank, broker, or government.

INVESTMENT BASICS

An investment involves risking your money in exchange for the possibility that those savings will increase before you need them. Investments may pay interest or dividends as well as offer opportunities for growth of your capital.

Using cash equivalents as an emergency or short-term savings vehicle illustrates that there are many facets to retirement planning. Because you're working for a goal of a financially secure retirement, you must invest—not merely save.

CASH EQUIVALENTS

Cash equivalents are short-term, interest earning securities that can be readily converted into cash with little or no change in the principal value. In other words, you get your original investment back—no more and no less—when you sell. Plus, of course, you receive interest along the way.

Treasury bills, for example, are offered at maturities of one year or less. Commercial paper, which is an obligation to pay a debt, is issued by top-rated corporations and typically has a maturity of 90 days or less.

The financial strength of most borrowers in the market for cash equivalents, such as government agencies, large corporations, and banks, combined with the short maturity of cash reserve investments means cash equivalents are essentially immune from significant market risk and interest rate risk.

Cash equivalent investments include money market accounts, money market funds, savings accounts, CDs, and Treasury bills.

All of the preceding investments provide stability of principal and offer interest rates that change periodically. The interest paid on cash-equivalent investments fluctuate when interest rates drop.

> **tip** Because the interest rates on cash equivalents are generally close to the inflation rate for the same period, they are best viewed as a temporary parking place for your money while you're waiting for a more attractive investment opportunity.

MONEY MARKET ACCOUNTS AND FUNDS

Don't confuse money market accounts offered by banks and Savings and Loan Associations (S&Ls) with money market funds offered by brokerage and mutual fund companies. Think of money market accounts as limited checking accounts (you can write only a few checks each month in most cases) that pay daily interest in relation to market rates.

Because money market accounts are offered by banks and S&Ls, these accounts carry Federal Deposit Insurance Corporation (FDIC) insurance up to $100,000 and are, thus, generally risk-free.

> **Money Market Fund.** An open-ended mutual fund that invests in commercial paper, bankers' acceptances, repurchase agreements, government securities, CDs, and other highly liquid and safe securities, and pays money market rates of interest. The fund's net asset value remains a constant $1 a share, only the interest rate goes up or down.

Unlike money market accounts, money market funds are not insured by a government agency. That should not cause much concern however. After all, these funds invest in the highest quality U.S. government securities, commercial paper, bankers' acceptances, and other securities. The funds also usually pay a higher rate of interest than bank money market accounts.

SAVINGS ACCOUNTS

If you save $100 per month in a basic savings account at your local bank for 30 years, earning five percent annually, your total will be $83,573 (without accounting for taxes). That includes $36,000 of principal that you invested plus $47,573 in earnings for that money.

BANK PAPER OR CDS

Banks and savings institutions may offer CDs at whatever amount, maturity, and interest rate they choose. This means that you can shop among banks to find the CD package that's best for your retirement plan.

In fact, because you can buy and redeem CDs by mail, it is just as easy to do business with a bank in another state as with one across the street. You can also purchase CDs from brokerage firms.

When investing in CDs, you should be aware of the following:

- If the interest rate a bank offers is substantially higher than the going rate for CDs of similar amounts and maturity, be skeptical. The bank may be in a shabby financial condition and forced to offer the higher rate in order to attract new money. If the bank is an FDIC institution, FDIC insurance would cover your loss if the bank failed—but not necessarily the interest due you. Not to mention having the money tied up for months.

- With CDs, you might also find out about getting
  your money back before the CD matures. In some
  cases, the bank or S&L can penalize you with an
  early withdrawal penalty, which could wipe out any
  interest due to you.

tip
You may not be hit with a penalty if you withdraw
your CD before its due date from a brokerage firm.
That's because these firms can often simply sell
your certificates to other investors.

U.S. TREASURY BILLS

Because Treasury bills (T-bills) are backed by the full faith and
credit of the U.S. government, there's no safer place for your
principal. In other words, T-bills are not insured like many
bank accounts, but the only way they will not be redeemed is
if the U.S. government goes belly-up.

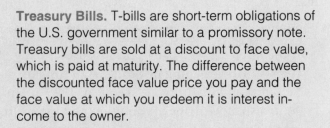

Treasury Bills. T-bills are short-term obligations of
the U.S. government similar to a promissory note.
Treasury bills are sold at a discount to face value,
which is paid at maturity. The difference between
the discounted face value price you pay and the
face value at which you redeem it is interest income to the owner.

With an investment in T-bills, you might worry about getting
your money back before the maturity period is up. Fortunately, that isn't a problem because T-bills are completely liquid. You can sell them through a broker at any time.

However, when you sell a T-bill before its maturity, you may realize a gain or loss, depending on whether current interest rates are higher or lower than the rate in effect when you bought the bill. You can purchase T-bills through a broker or a bank in denominations of $10,000 and higher, and thereafter in multiples of $5,000. Brokers and banks usually charge small fees, usually $25 to $50, per transaction. You can eliminate commission charges by buying T-bills directly from Federal Reserve banks or their branches.

For a free brochure on how to buy Treasury securities from a Federal Reserve bank or branch, write to

> Bureau of Public Debt
> Division of Customer Service
> 300 13th Street SW
> Washington, DC 20239-0001

In this lesson, you learned about using cash equivalents until more lucrative investment opportunities emerge. In the next lesson, you will learn about basic growth investments, stocks, and mutual funds.

GROWTH INVESTMENTS FOR YOUR RETIREMENT PORTFOLIO

In this lesson, you will learn about growth investments, including stocks and mutual funds, for your retirement portfolio.

THE IMPORTANCE OF GROWTH INVESTMENTS

Selecting growth in both individual stocks and in mutual funds means seeking companies that will generate above-average increases in earnings and will outperform the market in the long run. In other words, you want stocks and funds whose rate of future earnings growth is not yet reflected in their current prices.

USING STOCKS TO FORM THE NUCLEUS OF YOUR GROWTH INVESTMENTS

With 20 or 30 years to go until retirement and a need for investments that will continue to be used long after that retirement date, the nucleus of your retirement portfolio will, in all likelihood, consist of stocks. Thus, an important part of your portfolio will be in stocks.

Stock. Ownership of a corporation represented by shares that are a claim on the corporation's earnings and assets.

When you think of stock, you usually think of common stock, which represents an ownership share in the company that issued it. If you own stock in General Motors, for example, you own a proportional share (no matter how minuscule) of General Motors' vast network of factories and subsidiaries. You will share in General Motors' profits or, in some years, shoulder a portion of the company's losses. Of course, common stock may or may not pay dividends.

It should be noted that many companies pay dividends regardless of the company's performance; dividends are simply a distribution of company earnings to company owners (stockholders).

Dividends. Dividends (or yields) are what the company distributes to its owners/shareholders.

Although stocks specifically pay dividends, similar profits from other investments are often referred to as yield. Occasionally, you will see references to the yield of a stock or the yield of a particular type of investment.

Yield. If you divide the current annual dividend of any stock by the share price, you get the stock's yield.

Many companies also issue a special class of shares called pre-ferred stock. These shares generally pay a higher dividend than common stock, but don't have the same price-appreciation potential of common stock. They appeal mainly to corpora-tions that get tax breaks on their dividend income. Individuals don't get that break, so there's no good reason to include this more esoteric stock investment in your retirement portfolio.

TYPES OF STOCK

There are five basic (often overlapping) stock categories that you can consider for your retirement portfolio:

- **Growth Stocks.** These are called growth stocks because they have good prospects for growing faster than the economy or the stock market in general. Investors like them for their consistent earnings growth and the likelihood that share prices will go up significantly over the long term.

- **Blue-Chip Stocks.** This group is loosely defined. Many large growth stocks are also considered blue-chip stocks. Blue-chip stocks are generally industry-leading companies with top-shelf financial credentials. They tend to pay decent, steadily rising dividends, generate some growth, and offer safety and reliability.

  Blue-chip stocks may form your retirement portfolio's core holdings, which is a group of stocks that you plan to always hold while adding to your position as your portfolio grows.

- **Income Stocks.** These securities pay out a much larger portion of their profits (often as much as 50 to 80 percent) in the form of quarterly dividends to investors than do other stocks. These tend to be more mature, slower-growth companies, and the dividends paid to investors make these shares generally less risky to own than shares of growth or small company stocks.

Though share prices of income stocks aren't expected to grow rapidly, the dividend acts as a kind of cushion beneath the share price. Even if the market falls, income stocks are usually less affected because investors will still receive the dividend.

> ***tip*** Dividends are only one way that income stocks make money for your retirement nest egg. The key is their total return: the combination of dividends plus the growth in the price of the shares.

- **Small Company Stocks.** Shares in these companies are riskier than blue-chip or income stocks. But as a group, their long-term average returns are higher. Small company stocks are typically newer, fast-growing companies.

- **Foreign Stocks.** These investments also play a role in most retirement nest eggs. They're available through an array of foreign stock mutual funds. The two benefits of adding an international flavor to your nest egg are diversification and performance.

Looking beyond the U.S. market broadens your investment universe. That's essential in an age when your personal prosperity is closely linked to the prosperity of the world's economies.

Foreign shares help diversify your nest egg because international markets usually perform differently than the U.S. market does. When stocks in the U.S. are down, those in other countries may be rising. The reverse is also true, of course, but by investing in a mutual fund that owns stocks in many countries, you can reduce the effects of a downturn in any one foreign market.

> **!** Because of the currency risk of owning foreign stocks, most small investors are better off in an international mutual fund that spreads this risk among many countries and currencies.

Stocks and Long-Term Gains

Stocks are the best place to invest a long-term retirement nest egg. In the long-term performance race, stocks are winners by a big margin over virtually any time period chosen.

Stock Investing Tips

There are a few facts you should learn to ensure that your investments in the stock market pay off.

- Never buy stocks indiscriminately. Make investments only when you have a reason to buy them.

- Select a promising industry, one with a good outlook.

- Diversify—try to own stocks in several industries.

- Buy low and sell high—easily said but difficult to achieve.

- Stay abreast of market trends.

- Use stop-loss orders to protect against losses. Stop-loss orders fence in gains by restricting the effects of a market downturn on your stocks.

- Buy value. Companies with strong finances (not too much debt) and solid earnings growth are consistently better long-term purchases.

DON'T PICK STOCKS—PICK A MUTUAL FUND

For many investors, mutual funds offer some advantages over individual stocks.

 Mutual Fund. A mutual fund is a professionally managed investment company comprised of a pool of investors' money used to purchase a diversified portfolio of stocks, bonds, money market instruments, or other securities. Each share in a mutual fund represents a small slice of the mutual fund's total portfolio.

Mutual funds grew from just over $100 billion in assets in 1980 to more than $1.6 trillion in assets by 1993. The result is that, today, there are more than 3,400 mutual funds to choose from compared with about 500 just a decade ago.

There are several reasons why mutual funds have become such a popular investment:

- **It's easy to invest in them.** Most transactions can be completed on the phone. Often, you can make an initial investment of as little as $50.

- **Performance.** Because they are designed for growth of capital, performance can be quite good. The average stock mutual fund's annual rate of return over the past decade, for example, was almost 12 percent.

- **Less risk.** They provide a low-cost way to diversify your retirement investments, thereby reducing investment risk. Using professional management by experienced managers who are responsible for investing and managing the stock and/or bond holdings continuously risk is usually reduced.

MUTUAL FUND OPTIONS AND STRATEGIES

As with stocks, the type of mutual fund you invest in will depend on your needs, your goals, and your risk threshold. However, as with stock investments, there are a few tips and strategies that will help you make the most of your invested funds:

- Utilize the options offered by many mutual funds by automatically reinvesting dividends and capital gains. Many mutual funds automatically take all dividends and profits and immediately buy more shares of the fund for you. Reinvestment of dividends and capital gains is mandatory for retirement accounts until you reach the age of 59 and a half.

- Planned investment programs, such as periodic payment plans, make investing a contractual obligation similar to forced savings.

- The fact that most mutual funds are listed in newspapers makes it easy to keep tabs on performance.

- Like the securities that they invest in, a mutual fund's asset value will fluctuate with changing market conditions.

The commission and fee structure of mutual funds can be confusing. The funds range from no-load funds, which carry no sales commissions and are sold only to the public; to low-load funds, which have a commission of one to three percent; to load funds, which typically charge commissions of four to eight and a half percent.

Commission. Commission refers to a charge by the mutual fund for you to open an account, or take out investment.

Some funds assess a charge if you redeem your fund shares within a specified period of time. Some funds also charge a sales distribution fee each year you hold the fund.

MUTUAL FUND CATEGORIES

After you determine a proper category for your retirement funds, the individual funds within that category should be evaluated for performance, price, and so on.

Here are the major categories of mutual funds:

- **Stock Funds.** A stock (or equity) mutual fund invests its money in stocks of individual companies.

- **Bond Funds.** A bond mutual fund invests its money in bonds of companies or governments that are as varied as those that stock funds invest in.

- **Money Market Funds.** A money market fund invests its money in short-term financial instruments such as Treasury bills and CDs.

MUTUAL FUND TYPES

Within their respective categories, each mutual fund can also be classed according to type:

- **Open-End Mutual Funds.** These sell an unlimited number of new shares and constantly repurchase or redeem outstanding ones. The amount of money in the fund is always changing.

- **Closed-End Mutual Funds.** These have a relatively fixed amount of assets under management. Closed-end mutual funds raise money as ordinary companies do—with an initial offering on a recognized stock exchange. After they're issued, the shares of closed-end mutual funds are traded just like any other stock—on the major stock exchanges and over the counter.

- **Stock Exchange.** Organized marketplace in which stocks and bonds are traded by members of the exchange.

- **Over the Counter (OTC).** Market in which securities transactions are conducted through a telephone and computer network connecting dealers in stocks and bonds rather than on the floor of an exchange.

MUTUAL FUND SAFETY

Mutual funds are not insured or guaranteed by any government agency, but their operations are regulated by the U.S. Securities and Exchange Commission and by state agencies. The Investment Company Act of 1940, the principal Federal law regulating mutual funds, requires funds to operate in the interest of shareholders and to take steps to safeguard their assets.

Fund advisers must also provide extensive disclosure about their investment activities, risks, fees, and sales commissions.

MUTUAL FUND TAX STRATEGIES

If you're investing though a taxable investment account, put the emphasis on low-yielding growth funds rather than higher yielding funds. This will minimize your current taxable dividend income.

As you change your portfolio allocation, try to minimize the extent of capital gains realization from the rebalancing. It is always more tax-effective to adjust your asset allocation by adding new contributions to a lagging investment rather than selling an appreciated investment.

In this lesson, you learned that stocks and mutual funds will make up the bulk of your retirement plan investments. In the next lesson, you will learn about investing for income.

13

INCOME INVESTMENTS

In this lesson, you will learn that cash and fixed-income investments play an important role in any portfolio, especially when you get closer to retirement.

BONDS

Bonds provide a stable level of income and often reduce portfolio risk. Therefore, they should be part of portfolios for younger investors, albeit, a small part for investors under the age of 40.

> **Bond.** Bonds are loans in the form of a publicly traded security. An investor who buys a bond is making a loan for a certain number of years to the government agency, corporation, or other entity that issues the bond.

A bond is a fixed-income security because the interest paid, known as the coupon, is typically a fixed amount. A $1,000 bond issued with a seven percent coupon would pay a fixed $70 in interest each year.

While the coupon amount of the bond may be fixed, the price of a bond is not. As interest rates rise, bond prices will drop; falling interest rates cause bond prices to move upward. Investors will bid up or push down a bond's price until its yield to maturity is in line with market interest rates.

Bonds are attractive to investors for several reasons:

- They provide higher income than cash equivalents, such as Treasury bills or money market funds. Many investors who require current income to meet their living expenses allocate the bulk of their investment portfolio to bonds.

- Bond income is also highly predictable. If you purchase a government bond, you are assured of receiving payments of interest and principal when they come due.

DIVERSIFICATION

Bonds provide portfolio diversification, which can help dampen the effects of swings in stock prices. This is because bond prices, in general, do not correlate to the movement of stock prices; bond price swings are usually less volatile than stocks.

You don't have to worry about fluctuations in bond prices if your intent is to hold bond investments until they mature. Unlike stocks, bonds have a maturity date at which point the bond issuer will return the principal at par value.

Par Value. The stated or face value of a stock or bond. It has little significance for common stock. The par value on bonds specifies the payment at maturity.

In the meantime, swings in interest rates may cause your bond's price to rise above or fall below par, but you don't need to worry. You can be assured of getting your money back as long as the bond issuer is creditworthy. This applies to individual bonds but not to bond market funds because mutual funds do not have a particular maturity date when principal is returned.

GOVERNMENT BONDS

Certain government agencies also issue securities and bonds. Some of the bonds are explicitly guaranteed by the U.S. government. However, all are considered safe because, even without an express guarantee, the risk of default is considered extremely low.

The best known types of government securities are mortgage pools, which are pools of home mortgages issued by the government National Mortgage Association (GNMA or Ginnie Mae), Federal National Mortgage Association (FNMA or Fannie Mae), and Federal Home Loan Mortgage Corporation (FHLMC or Freddie Mac).

These entities all buy mortgages from banks and thrifts (a generic name for savings banks and savings and loan associations), pool them, and then sell units of the pools to investors creating a safe haven for some of your retirement portfolio.

GINNIE MAES

When you buy Ginnie Maes, you're actually purchasing a portion of the 30-year mortgages issued by the U.S. Federal Housing Administration (FHA) and the Veterans Administration (VA). The GNMA collects monthly interest and principal payments that homeowners pay on their mortgages, subtracts a small administrative fee, and passes the payments on to its investors.

Because homeowners' monthly payments include both principal and interest, the check that investors receive each month includes both interest income and some principal. Only the interest portion, of course, is taxable. The amount of principal and interest a Ginnie Mae pays each month fluctuates because some homeowners pay off their mortgages (they sell or refinance their homes). So, if you invest in Ginnie Maes, you can't predict precisely how much you'll receive each month.

FANNIE MAES AND FREDDIE MACS

Fannie Maes and Freddie Macs are also mortgage-backed securities based on government funding for housing. These securities make regular interest payments but you don't receive your principal until the securities mature.

Fannie Maes and Freddie Macs carry more risk than Ginnie Maes because they invest in mortgages that aren't insured by the FHA or VA. Even though the mortgage isn't guaranteed, however, the FNMA and the FHLMC do guarantee that you will receive your interest payments. Because these securities are riskier, they can pay a higher rate of interest than a Ginnie Mae.

BASIC TREASURY SECURITIES

Treasury securities are the means by which the U.S. government borrows money. Treasury bills, notes, and bonds are issued regularly by the Federal Reserve and are a popular investment for people who want very little principal risk.

> *tip* Because these are direct obligations of the U.S. government, the interest on Treasury bills, notes, and bonds is usually exempt from state income taxes.

Treasury bills are cash-equivalent debt instruments issued at various maturities; auctions of 90-day and the 182-day bills take place weekly. The U.S. Treasury also auctions 52-week bills once every four weeks.

Treasury bills are issued in minimum denominations of $10,000, and subsequent purchases may be made at $5,000 increments. Treasury bills are sold at a discount from the face (maturity) value. The amount of that discount is equal to the interest that will be paid at maturity. Therefore, upon maturity, the investor receives the face value of the Treasury bill.

Treasury notes and bonds are fixed-income obligations that have longer terms and pay interest semiannually at a fixed interest rate. They are sold at face value.

ZERO-COUPON BONDS

An interesting type of U.S. Treasury security is the zero-coupon bond. These bonds pay no interest along the way. Instead, they are sold at a deep discount or at a price that is much lower than the maturity value of the bond.

Because you don't get any interest during the holding period, your profit comes at maturity in the form of a large increase in the amount you receive.

The main advantage of zero-coupon bonds is that you're guaranteed a set return at the original interest rates. Therefore, if interest rates decline, you don't have to worry about reinvesting interest income at a lower rate. This automatic compounding also allows you to avoid having to decide on reinvesting the interest you would receive on a regular bond, one consideration with retirement planning.

> **!** Even though you are not receiving interest along the way, the IRS assumes that you are for income tax purposes, so you have to pay income taxes on that imputed interest income. In a retirement account, however, this assumed income is irrelevant for current tax purposes.

TAX-DEFERRAL AND GOVERNMENT SECURITIES

Tax deferral and other types of government securities are good investments for retirement accounts, such as IRAs and Keogh plans, because taxes are deferred until you withdraw the income at a later date.

CORPORATE BONDS

Corporate bonds are riskier than bonds issued by the U.S. government. If the company issuing your bond fails, your ability to get your money back depends on the provisions of the bond you buy.

Bondholders do not usually take priority over common stockholders when a company's assets are distributed. In practice, however, few people below the level of secured creditor receive any return of principal when a company goes bankrupt. As you might expect, to compensate for this extra risk, corporate bonds pay higher yields than government bonds.

> **tip** Most corporations issue bonds in denominations of $1,000, but you must buy them in lots of five. However, you can invest in a bond mutual fund, where the initial investment requirements can be as low as $250. By investing in a bond mutual fund, you'll have a very diversified bond portfolio because you'll own a share of probably 50 to 100 different bonds.

Unlike municipal bonds, which you'll learn more about in Lesson 14, the interest you earn on corporate bonds is subject to federal, state, and local taxes. Corporate bonds are liquid, however. You can usually sell them without too much trouble before they mature. Bonds that carry the highest ratings are the most liquid.

HIGH-YIELD BONDS

A high-yield bond is a unique type of corporate bond known in the trade as a "junk bond." These investments pay very high yields and for a good reason—the risk you take when you purchase the bond is very high.

If the company goes bankrupt, you'll probably lose every penny you invest. Recently, defaults on these low-grade corporate bonds occurred more frequently than defaults on other corporate bonds. The outlook for these bonds is highly dependent on the state of the economy.

In this lesson, you learned how income investments fit into your retirement portfolio. In the next lesson, you will learn about tax-free investments and the annuity that can be both tax-deferred savings and insurance.

14

TAX-FREE AND TAX-DEFERRED INCOME INVESTMENTS

In this lesson, you will learn more about tax-free and tax-deferred investments and how they fit into your retirement portfolio.

THE ROLE OF TAX-EXEMPT INVESTMENTS

Obviously, as you build up your retirement portfolio, you should be looking for ways to reduce your tax liability.

Tax-Exempt Investments. Tax-exempt investments are investments designed so the interest they pay is free from federal taxes, and even from state and local taxes in some cases.

> **tip** Consider investing in tax-free securities, such as municipal securities, if your taxable income is expected to place you in the 28-percent tax bracket or higher.

MUNICIPAL SECURITIES

> **Municipal Securities.** Municipal securities (or munis) are debt obligations issued by state and local government agencies, such as a highway department, an airport authority, a school district, or a sewer commission.

Debt obligations are interest-paying IOUs that raise money for many state or local government purposes. State and local governments issue debt obligations for a variety of reasons, which gives you many options to choose from.

> **tip** The interest on most municipals is usually exempt from federal taxes. That interest is exempt from state and local taxes if you're a resident of the state that issues the debt.

> **!** One risk of using either individual municipal bonds or shares in a municipal bond fund is that if interest rates rise, the value of the securities may decline. This is known as interest rate risk. If interest rates decline, the value of the municipal bonds or the share price of a municipal bond fund investment may increase.

CAPITAL GAINS TAXES

Capital gains that may be realized when a municipal security is sold will be subject to federal and most state capital gains taxes.

 Capital Gains. Capital gains are gains on the sale of a capital asset. Since 1991, the maximum individual tax rate on capital gain has been 28 percent.

DOUBLE TAX-FREE SECURITIES

Investors who hold municipal securities of issuers located within their own state get a double benefit: interest on these bonds or notes is free from both federal and state taxes.

TAX-EXEMPT FUNDS

If you're in the highest tax bracket, the potentially higher after-tax yields of municipals, money market funds, and municipal bond funds may make them appropriate alternatives to taxable funds. Municipal funds typically pay lower pretax yields than taxable funds, but their "tax adjusted" yields should be superior for high tax bracket investors.

Interest income from municipal bond funds is generally exempt from federal income taxes. In addition, if a fund invests primarily in the debt obligations of the state in which you reside, the fund's dividend income will be exempt from state and local taxes as well.

> ***tip*** While dividend income from municipal funds escapes federal taxation, capital gains distributions do not. They are fully taxable at the federal level and may be subject to state and local taxes as well.

U.S. TREASURY SECURITIES FUNDS

One final tax exemption worth noting applies to funds that invest in U.S. Treasury securities. All income that is derived from U.S. Treasury obligations is exempt from state and local taxes in every state. Unfortunately, federal income taxes will still apply to U.S. Treasury income—but the high income taxes of many states may make these funds worth investigating.

TAX-DEFERRED INVESTMENTS

The IRS looks favorably on working people who set aside money for retirement via 401(k) plans, 403(b) plans, IRAs, and so on, by allowing such savings to grow free of tax until the money is withdrawn. In many cases, the money you originally contributed to those plans is not currently subject to federal income tax.

tip   Anyone with earned income should consider establishing an IRA. Anyone with income from self-employment should consider contributing to a self-employed retirement account, such as a Keogh or SEP plan. And anyone whose employers offer a 401(k) plan or a thrift plan should be sure to participate to the maximum extent.

Annuities

Annuities are life insurance with a twist. While life insurance protects your dependents in the event of your death, an annuity covers the risk that you will live longer than expected. An annuity pays you a fixed amount of money each year for the rest of your life, regardless of how long you live.

Annuities. An annuity is a tax-deferred investment contract that is underwritten by an insurance company. Although annuities come in a variety of types, the two primary types are immediate annuities and deferred annuities.

With an immediate annuity, you usually purchase the contract with a lump sum and begin receiving benefits 30 to 90 days later. A deferred annuity, on the other hand, pays you benefits starting at some future date, usually at retirement.

You buy your annuity contract by paying a lump sum, by making installment payments, or by some combination of the two. With a fixed annuity, the amount you receive is paid out in regular equal installments. You decide how frequently you want to receive payments (monthly, quarterly, or annually). That payment can be over a fixed period, such as 20 years, or for the rest of your life.

The most popular annuity for retirement investors is a variable deferred annuity. Variable annuities allow you to invest in a portfolio of investment options (such as guaranteed interest contracts or bond and stock mutual funds) that you select. With a variable annuity, the interest, dividends, and capital gains you earn accumulate tax-deferred until they're paid to you under the terms of your annuity.

> **!** The price for an early withdrawal from an annuity is the same 10 percent penalty assessed on premature withdrawals from IRAs, Keoghs, and similar tax-deferred investments. You will pay ordinary income taxes plus a 10 percent penalty if you take the money out before age 59 and a half.

Annuities have their advantages if you want tax-deferred growth, but can sometimes be a very expensive way to buy your investments. In addition to any sales commissions you pay to get in, these contracts (like mutual funds) charge investment management fees and have administrative costs. And, because they also offer a death benefit, these contracts charge for the life insurance protection.

There may also be surrender charges imposed if you take funds out of the contract too soon. All of these fees are in addition to those charged by the funds.

In this lesson, you learned about the role of tax-free municipal bonds and annuities. In the next lesson, you will learn about other investments that may provide you with long-term growth.

15

ASSET
ALLOCATION

In this lesson, you will learn the importance of allocating the assets you already possess and those you will acquire as you work toward your retirement goal.

ALLOCATING YOUR RETIREMENT ASSETS

Savvy investors initially put aside considerations of which individual mutual fund, which stocks, or which hard assets to own and focus on their portfolio allocation.

Asset Allocation. This is the process of dividing your investable assets among the investment categories in the most appropriate manner given your retirement goals, your need for current income, and the time horizon you have until you will need the invested money.

PROPER ALLOCATION

How do you determine the proper allocation for your unique situation? There are four basic factors you should consider:

- **Your tolerance for risk.** This is often called the sleep-at-night factor. Risk tolerance can be hard to measure because it involves complex psychological factors. Only you know how you feel about risk, but most people are very risk-adverse by nature and don't want to lose money.

- **Your age and investment horizon.** This is probably the most critical factor because your time horizon to a particular goal governs the amount of risk you should take with your investments. It is also a major factor in the rate of return you will need in order to achieve your goal. With many years until retirement, you can afford riskier investments.

- **The phase of your investment cycle (accumulation or distribution).** If you're in the accumulation phase, you can have more growth-oriented investments in your portfolio and still manage market risk. On the other hand, if you need current income, you don't want to be selling your growth-oriented investments in volatile markets simply because of a need to generate current income.

- **Other factors, such as large concentrations in company stock.** Sometimes, corporate employees have large amounts of company stock that they don't want to sell due to the company's potential or other factors. Asset allocation should take into account the need for additional diversification within the equity category given the large amount of business risk these individuals will be taking.

Personal Risk Tolerance

Your asset allocation decisions will be influenced by your attitude towards investment risk. Because perceptions of risk vary from one investor to the next, two individuals with essentially identical profiles—the same income levels, same financial goals, same Social Security benefits, and the same level of savings—may choose to adopt quite different asset allocations.

Investment Horizon

You can measure your investment horizon in the scale of a human life span. On average, most individuals who reach the traditional retirement age of 65 will live into their 80s. Thus, when you begin to save for retirement in your 20s or 30s, you should anticipate an investment span or horizon of 50 to 60 years.

tip Even after you reach your 40s and 50s, you still have an investment horizon of three to four decades. As you age, your investment horizon obviously diminishes so that by the time you reach your 80s, it may extend 10 years or less. But if you plan to leave a portion of your retirement savings to your heirs, your investment horizon will extend well beyond your own life span.

When you're figuring your investment horizon, an important factor to consider is your own family history. If members of your family have lived into their 90s and you (and your spouse) are in good health, you probably should plan on your investment horizon extending through age 100.

YOUR PERSONAL FINANCIAL RESOURCES

Your personal financial situation will be the final factor that influences your asset allocation decisions. If you feel that your financial situation is tenuous (for example, if your company has been experiencing layoffs), you may want to reduce your investment risk.

However, if your finances are on a sound footing, you may be able to assume a higher level of investment risk because you have so long before retirement to recoup any losses.

ASSET ALLOCATION FUNDS

Asset allocation mutual funds perform the allocation function for you by investing in stocks, bonds, money markets, real estate markets, and more so that any one market's losses may be offset by another's gain.

ESOPS AND ASSET ALLOCATION

Owning stock in your employer's company can leave your asset allocation seriously out of balance. For example, if your employer's stock represents 50 percent of the value of your total investments and if you have decided that the appropriate asset allocation for your portfolio should be 50 percent stocks, 40 percent bonds, and 10 percent hard assets, should you not own any other stocks?

In other words, it is best to apply your asset allocation breakdown to your other assets, virtually ignoring the amounts invested in ESOPs because of their potential to seriously warp your portfolio.

In this example, you would divide the half of your portfolio that is not employer stock according to 50-40-10 allocation of stocks, bonds, and hard assets to allow for sufficient diversity in your stock investments.

Investment Objectives

In investment terms, your objective during the accumulation years is to achieve growth of your capital; your emphasis during the distributive years of retirement shifts to income generation plus a sufficient level of capital growth to protect against inflation. Along with your primary long-term retirement objectives, you should have a secondary objective as well: short-term liquidity.

Most financial planners recommend that, in addition to your long-term retirement savings, you should maintain an emergency fund in a nonretirement account equal to three to six months of living expenses during your working years and six months' to one year's worth of living expenses during your retirement years.

For People Age 30 and Younger

If you're in your early and middle working years and your investment horizon extends 40 years or more, your primary investment objectives should be to accumulate capital for your retirement.

At this point in your life, common stocks should be your dominant investment option. Stocks have provided the highest long-term total return of any major asset class and, while stocks also have the highest volatility level of any asset class, the passage of time has a dampening effect on their short-term fluctuations.

Although a 100 percent stock portfolio may be appropriate for accumulation investors in the earliest stages of the investment life cycle, few investors should commit all of their savings to stocks.

tip   For most investors, it is probably wise to maintain a modest investment in bonds as well. The recommended allocation during the accumulation years is 80 percent stock and 20 percent bonds.

Early Retirement Years

In this situation, it seems appropriate to reduce your common stock commitment while moving some of your assets into shorter-term reserves. Your recommended asset allocation would be 40 percent stocks, 40 percent bonds, and 20 percent short-term reserves. With 20 or 30 years to live after retirement, a higher percentage of stocks still makes sense.

In this lesson, you learned how to allocate your retirement assets based on your position in the life cycle. In the next lesson, you will begin to learn about the various investment strategies that can help you profit from the allocation of assets that best fits your individual situation.

16

INVESTMENT STRATEGIES

In this lesson, you will learn how to use investing strategies to maximize the growth of your assets, whether you invest on your own or use professional money managers.

INVESTMENT FUNDAMENTALS

Many investors don't fully understand the fundamentals of investing and therefore may have unrealistic expectations about an investment's future performance. For example, money market mutual funds represent a low-risk haven for emergency reserves and should not be expected to match the performance of more volatile bonds. Likewise, bonds or bond funds should not be expected to generate the capital growth that you need, if you're planning to retire in 20 years or longer.

While the steady decline in interest rates that began in the mid-1980s has resulted in substantial capital returns for bond funds, inexperienced investors may view these yield-driven price gains as a sustainable component of the investment returns on bond funds. When interest rates reverse their protracted decline, these investors may be severely disappointed.

When it comes to stocks and stock mutual funds, don't be fooled into believing that the +15 percent annual returns earned on stock investments during the past decade are normal. In fact, these returns are well above the 10 percent historical average.

After you understand how to analyze an investment's past performance records and its expected role in your retirement plan, you must learn about investment strategies and how they apply to those investments you selected to allocate to your retirement assets.

When it comes to investing in stocks, there are a number of strategies that you should learn. For example, here are some strategies you should learn to understand the basics of common stock investments:

- You can't forecast day-to-day price changes. Most stocks merely move in the direction of the overall market. Developments in a particular industry may also affect the prices of stocks in that sector.

- Over the long term, there's an uncanny correlation between share price and a company's profitability. Given this link, it is important to focus on a company's profits (also called earnings) before investing in any stock. The size of a company's profits alone won't tell you much. What is important are profits in relation to the number of shares outstanding—in other words, earnings per share (EPS).

- Dividing earnings by the average number of common stock shares outstanding during the period being measured gives you the EPS figure. Look for companies with a pattern of EPS growth over at least five years and a habit of reinvesting 35 percent or more of earnings in expansion of the business.

> *tip* You can determine the reinvestment rate by comparing earnings per share with the dividend payment. Earnings that aren't paid out to shareholders get reinvested in the business.

PRICE-EARNINGS RATIO

Stocks are not all equally valued. You can get an idea of which are cheap and which are expensive by checking how each stock is priced in relation to its earnings. A key measure of a stock's price compared with others is its price-earnings ratio (P/E).

The P/E is an indication of whether a stock is cheap or expensive, and is probably the single most important number that you can know about a stock.

> **P/E.** The price-earnings ratio (or P/E) is the price of a share divided by the company's earnings per share. If a stock sells for $35 per share and the company earned $3.50 per share for the previous 12 months, the stock has a P/E ratio of 10. The P/E indicates how much investors are willing to pay for each dollar per share that the company earns.

The easiest way to find a company's P/E ratio is in the newspaper stock tables alongside the stock's price. Unfortunately, what you see may not be too useful. The numbers may reflect one-time factors, such as earnings write-offs or asset sales, that temporarily deflate or inflate a company's profitability.

Another problem is that P/E ratios in newspapers are based on the previous 12 months' earnings, whereas the investment world looks ahead. In other words, real pros calculate a company's P/E using forecasts of its profits over the next year and sometimes longer.

There is no hard-and-fast rule for interpreting P/E ratios. You can, however, use these analytical techniques:

- **Think small.** A low P/E may indicate an undervalued stock. Over long periods, stocks with low P/Es deliver surprising returns. But there's no rule that says that a cheap stock won't simply get cheaper. If you invest in low P/E stocks, make sure you're comfortable that the earnings part of the equation won't let you down.

- **Look at similar stocks.** If most drug companies have P/Es of 20 but one trades for a P/E of 16, then (with all other things being equal) that one might be undervalued. Naturally, you don't want to make such comparisons of companies in dissimilar industries.

- **Compare growth with P/E.** You'll rarely see a company with steadily increasing earnings and a below-average P/E ratio because investors "pay up" for the likelihood that the company will deliver high profits. Those profits will later lower the P/E based on today's price.

BOND STRATEGIES

Bonds can't match the performance record of stocks over the long haul. But they have performed well over shorter time periods—particularly since the 1980s. Because bonds should play a role in your retirement plans, you should consider a number of bond purchase techniques:

- The ideal time to buy bonds is when interest rates have stabilized at a relatively high level or when they seem about to head down.

- Diversify by acquiring bonds with different maturity dates or bond funds with different average maturities. Short- and intermediate-term issues fluctuate less in price than long-term issues, and they don't require you to tie up your money for 10 or more years in exchange for a small additional yield.

- Don't buy any bond with a safety rating less than A and watch for news that may affect the rating while you own the bond.

tip To check the rating of any bond you're considering, ask your broker or look it up in any one of several bond guides found in many libraries (such as Moody's and Standard & Poors).

- For maximum safety, stick with bonds issued by the U.S. Treasury.

tip To buy Treasury bonds commission free, set up an account through a program called Treasury Direct. For details, contact your nearest Federal Reserve bank branch or call the Bureau of Public Debt, in Washington, DC, at 202-874-4000 (or write to U.S. Department of the Treasury, 1500 Pennsylvania Avenue, Washington, DC 20220).

- Watch for the bond's call provisions. Some bonds can be called, which means that they can be redeemed by the issuer before they mature.

> A company might decide to call its bonds if, for example, interest rates fall so far that it could issue new bonds at a lower price thus saving money. Call prices are good for the issuer but bad for investors. Not only would you lose comparatively high yield, you would also have to figure out where to invest the unexpected payment. Treasury issues are generally not callable.

MUTUAL FUND STRATEGIES

If you're planning your retirement before age 40, you'll want to consider using mutual funds. They let small investors hire professional money managers to take over the grunt work of investing—wading through reports on thousands of individual companies to compile a suitable investment portfolio.

With more than 4,500 mutual funds available today, how do you choose the one best suited to your needs?

Begin by comparing the fund's 5- and 10-year returns. You want to see how the fund you're considering has performed in both bull and bear markets. When you evaluate the risk associated with the historical return, you're really looking at the fund's volatility.

Bull. A person who thinks prices will rise.

Bear. A person who thinks market prices will fall.

Volatility. The susceptibility to rapid and extreme fluctuations in price.

The foundation of your retirement portfolio should consist of a diversified equity fund invested in U.S. common stocks and a diversified bond fund invested in investment-grade U.S. bonds.

Return and risk matter most when it comes to selecting a mutual fund. But you may not want to be aware of other factors, such as the fund's turnover rate (which is the average length of time that the fund holds shares before selling them).

A high turnover rate sometimes indicates that the fund manager is trying to time the market (that is, judge when the market is going up or down)—and market timing just doesn't work consistently.

In this lesson, you learned some of the basic investing strategies you will need to help your assets grow between now and retirement. In the next lesson, you will learn more strategies that can help you increase the profits from your investments.

MORE INVESTMENT STRATEGIES

In this lesson, you will learn about investment strategies that can help you make the most of your retirement assets. You will also learn more about the degree of risk you can tolerate in your retirement portfolio.

RISK VERSUS RETURN

Given the long time period that you have if you begin planning for your retirement before age 40, you could accept a lesser investment return and still reach your financial goal. However, as you get nearer to your planned retirement date, you may find yourself pressed to seek a higher return to attain your goal.

Because time is on your side, it therefore makes more sense to take more risk and hopefully achieve more return. Implicit in that trade-off is the notion of risk. With a higher expected return comes a greater level of risk.

Return. Return is the gain (earnings) you make on an investment.

With a bank savings account, for example, your return is the amount of interest you collect. The principal is guaranteed not to vary, so there's no gain or loss in value to add to the return equation.

On the other hand, when you buy a corporate bond, the price may rise or fall before you sell it. In that case, your return would have two elements: the amount of interest you receive plus or minus any gain or loss on the bond's price if it is sold before maturity. Risk is a bit more difficult to define.

 Risk. Risk is generally equated with a price fluctuation or, more accurately, the volatility of total return.

Slight changes in return up or down each year denote lower risk, while wider swings constitute higher risk. One common measure of investment volatility is called standard deviation. It's a statistic that measures the degree to which a series of annual returns varies above and below its average. The more volatile the investment, the larger the standard deviation.

MARKET RISK

 Market Risk. This is the danger that financial markets can rise or fall in value. As they do, the markets affect the value of a particular investment in the market even though the other risk factors for that investment may remain unchanged.

You may buy the stock of a prosperous company, for example, but the entire market may fall as a result of uncertainties about the economy. While your company may be doing quite well, investors will become wary of stocks in general, so the price of your stock will fall due to less demand.

You can protect yourself from volatility by investing for the long term. Over long periods, the stock market's ups and downs have been more moderate.

> ! The converse of investing for the long term is to try to eliminate market risk by "timing the market" (predicting where it is going and reacting accordingly). Generally, people who try to determine market changes (often called "market timers") do not consistently make the right call. In essence, market timing is sophisticated guessing.

PURCHASING POWER RISK

The biggest risk to your long-term retirement security is purchasing power risk.

> **Purchasing Power Risk.** Purchasing power risk is the risk that your money won't keep pace with inflation.

To reduce purchasing power risk, you should invest for the long term in assets whose returns have traditionally outpaced inflation, such as common stocks. You should invest to maintain a "real" rate of return over your investment time horizon.

How do you calculate your real return? Figure your after-tax rate of return and then subtract the current rate of inflation. The result is your real rate of return.

> **tip** By focusing on your real rate of return, you can calculate whether your investments are staying ahead of inflation. Investment experts point out that a one to four percent real rate of return in a moderately risky portfolio mix is a significant accomplishment.

BUYING TECHNIQUES

There are two basic market timing techniques used by investors:

- Dollar cost averaging
- Fixed amount investing

 Dollar Cost Averaging. This is a strategy of investing the same dollar amount in the same investment at fixed time intervals.

 Fixed Amount Investing. This is the strategy of keeping a constant dollar amount invested at certain time intervals, such as six months or one year.

If you're investing in individual stocks, these timing techniques may not be practical. However, they can be quite useful for timing mutual fund investments.

Investors usually have the option of investing in mutual funds in relatively small dollar amounts. You can make an agreement with a fund to send a fixed dollar amount every month to that fund. This adds discipline to your savings strategy. It also helps you establish a better cost basis for the fund.

When you send a fixed dollar amount every month, you will buy fewer shares when the price of shares goes up and more shares when the price goes down. You end up dollar cost averaging your price per share.

If the investment goes through a down cycle, you will be buying more shares while it is down, thus reducing the average cost per share over that time. If it goes up, you will be buying fewer shares at the higher price.

> **!** You should note that if the price of the investment only goes up after the initial investment, you would end up cost averaging a higher price per share— but it would still be profitable, of course.

Using fixed amount investing, you would sell shares if the total amount of the investment went over the original amount you put in and you would buy more shares if it went down.

ECONOMIC CYCLES

Fundamental analysis deals primarily with forecasting economic trends and cycles. If your total net worth isn't also expanding at the same rate as the economy, your percentage of the economy is shrinking.

Economic Cycle. An economic cycle is a period of either sustained inflation or recession.

Inflation. Inflation means that the price of most goods and services is rising and the size of the total economic base is expanding.

Recession. Recession is a downturn in economic activity, defined by many economists as two consecutive quarters of decline in a country's gross domestic product.

INVESTMENT STRATEGIES

There are two generally accepted theories of analysis of investments: fundamental and technical.

Fundamental Analysis. The basic premise of fundamental analysis is that the most important consideration for selecting a good stock for investment is the future earnings potential of the company. To forecast a particular company's earnings, however, you must also take into account the outlook for the economy as a whole and the outlook for the industry in which that company is involved.

Technical Analysis. This is a method of selecting good investments primarily on the basis of supply and demand factors. Technical analysis also relies heavily on interpreting chart patterns of the past performance of the stock's price.

Fundamental Analysis

Reading and analyzing financial statements and studying economic cycles and industry trends are disciplines of fundamental analysis. The single most important factor in fundamental analysis is the direction of interest rates. If you want to be a student of the stock market, you must first be a student of interest rates. Professional fund managers may argue this point; usually earnings are most important to a fundamentalist.

tip   As is the case with bonds, there is generally a direct cause-and-effect inverse relationship between interest rates and stock prices. As interest rates rise, stock prices drop. This is due, in part, to the fact that a rise in interest rates will generally result in a decrease in many companies' earnings.

Technical Analysis

Technical analysis involves methods of studying indicators that are intended to predict whether the supply of shares which will be offered for sale will be satisfied by the expected demand for those shares.

Most investors use fundamental analysis to select what to invest in, and they use technical analysis to help them decide when to invest in it.

In this lesson, you learned about the strategies used when you're investing. In the next lesson, you will learn how to use these strategies to keep track of your retirement assets.

MONITORING THROUGH RETIREMENT

In this lesson, you will learn that retirement planning is an ongoing process. It requires monitoring and fine-tuning up to and during retirement.

CONSIDER THE VITAL SIGNS

Setting your retirement plan in motion is the hardest part. Once you have set your retirement plan in motion, you have to make certain the plan stays on track. To do that, you'll have to constantly monitor your plan.

REASSESS WHENEVER NECESSARY

A job change, a big promotion, an inheritance, a divorce or marriage, a child who wants to attend an expensive private college, are all situations that can change the shape of your retirement finances. To keep your plan on track, recalculate your retirement income goal and the assets that you have to meet that goal whenever a major life change happens.

> **tip** It's a good idea to recalculate every few years even if there haven't been any big changes.

DIVORCE

No matter what your age, the pension you've accumulated at work will probably be considered an asset to be divided with your spouse if you are divorced. If you untie the knot at age 50, for example, a portion of the benefits you stand to collect at retirement could belong to your ex-spouse under what is known among divorce lawyers as a "qualified domestic relations order," or QDRO (pronounced kwa-dro). If you divorce at an earlier age, the amount you have begun to build in that pension plan may not be sufficient to worry about dividing.

> **tip** You may be able to collect a portion of your ex's pension from his or her employer.

DEATH OF A SPOUSE

After the death of a spouse, there are a number of steps you should take, such as the following:

- Revise your insurance coverage.
- Besides reviewing and changing the beneficiary designations on existing policies, you have to assess your own insurance needs as a result of the changed circumstances.

- If you were formerly covered as a spouse under a health insurance plan, continuing coverage will have to be arranged. Appropriate coverage will have to be acquired.

- Appropriate coverage in your name for auto, home-owner or renters, and umbrella liability insurance is also necessary.

- Depending on individual circumstances, you may need to adjust or increase the limits on disability and life insurance coverage.

CHECK SOCIAL SECURITY

Part of your ongoing monitoring of your retirement plan should involve those Social Security benefits that you will become entitled to at age 62 or later. You should occasionally check your Social Security records for mistakes and request a change if you find any.

tip   Call 800-772-1213 to request Form 7004-SM, the Request for Earnings and Benefits Estimate statement. Do this every three to five years.

PERFORMANCE TRACKING

It is vitally important to continue monitoring your retirement portfolio and all the investments you own. After all, it is a long way until your retirement and quite a bit can change.

You shouldn't be a fanatic about it; you don't have to check the stock and mutual fund tables every day. After all, this is a long-term proposition and paying too close attention can be just as damaging as ignoring it completely.

SAVINGS AND DEBT SCHEDULES

Damaging debt in the form of credit card balances can sap funds that could otherwise go to retirement savings. Watch those plastic balances to avoid paying unnecessary interest and channel the savings into your nest egg.

> **tip** You might even consider a plan to pay off your home mortgage early and save thousands of dollars in interest costs.

MONITOR YOUR COMPANY

Your own retirement plan may be closely linked to your company's health. That is especially true if you participate in a profit-sharing plan at work, hold any of your retirement assets in company stock, or participate in an employee stock ownership plan (ESOP).

You should read the company's annual and quarterly reports as well as outside media or analyst reports on the firm. If the company's growth prospects dim and other investment options are available for that money, consider switching your assets elsewhere.

In this lesson, you learned the importance of monitoring your retirement plan and the assets that form such an important part of it. In the next lesson, you will learn how to plan for the one circumstance you can't do anything about: death.

WHEN RETIREMENT IS IN SIGHT

In this lesson, you will learn that you shouldn't relax your planning efforts as you approach your planned retirement age.

EVALUATING AN EARLY RETIREMENT OFFER

What should you do if you receive such an early retirement offer? Obviously, if the offer comes early in life, you have the added option of accepting your employer's offer and seeking work elsewhere. Of course, you will still have to consider any of your retirement assets that may be invested in that company's benefit plans. You'll have to do some fast calculations.

BUYOUT OFFER

The terms of every early retirement offer vary depending on whether it's a true voluntary early retirement program or an involuntary severance program. Many voluntary early retirement offers provide employees with a host of benefits, from cash severance payments and enhanced pensions to post-retirement medical coverage and offers of counseling or help in finding a new job.

> *tip* Check the specifics of your retirement offer. Remember, your company has no legal obligation to offer these payments and its program may be very different.

EARLY RETIREMENT OFFERS

> *tip* Keep in mind that you do have a choice. Under federal law, you can't be forced to take the package that's offered. However, nothing prevents your company from later eliminating your job, demoting you, or otherwise making you wish you had taken the offer.

Many companies follow up voluntary programs with a less generous involuntary severance program within a year or two. Assuming you're under the age of 40, chances are you will choose to or have to continue working if you leave your current employer. If you receive an early retirement offer, think about your odds of landing another job.

CAN YOU AFFORD TO RETIRE YET?

If you have good prospects for finding another job or for starting your own business, the decision may become easier. For many, the real question comes down to whether you can afford to retire now. Consider the following issues if you receive an early retirement offer:

- Will you get lower benefits because you're retiring early or do enhanced age and years of service make up the difference?

- Will you receive enough to fund your retirement adequately until you qualify for Social Security benefits?

- How do your early retirement benefits compare with those that you would collect if you continued to work for your company?

PENSION DISTRIBUTION OPTIONS

When you're separated from your employer, you will be faced with a decision about the money you have invested in that company's benefits plans. That means removing those funds from the company benefit plan and not paying the entire amount over to the government in the form of taxes. That means you must qualify for a tax-free rollover of those funds.

TAX-FREE ROLLOVERS

While many company-sponsored benefit plans offer a choice between an annuity when you retire or lump-sum distributions, all 401(k) plans provide only for lump-sum distributions. Thus, you are likely to have at least one lump-sum distribution to deal with at the time you retire.

> *tip* With lump-sum distributions, your main advantage is flexibility. A lump sum gives you many choices related to how you invest your money and pay your taxes. You also have an opportunity to leave your heirs a lump sum of money that isn't available with a pension annuity.

LUMP-SUM TAXES

When it comes to income taxes, you can pay them up front when you receive the distribution and you may get a significant tax break if you qualify for forward averaging. Or, you can roll over your funds into a rollover IRA and postpone paying your taxes until you take the money out of the IRA.

You can also combine your choices: roll over part of the lump-sum distribution to an IRA and defer taxes on that portion, and pay taxes on the portion you don't roll over.

If you aren't retiring, only changing jobs, you might be able to simply transfer the lump sum to your new employer's plan.

> **!** If you take the money yourself and do not use a direct rollover, do not miss the 60-day deadline. If you do, there is a 20 percent tax withholding when the money goes from the plan directly to you. Plus, you lose the right to roll your distribution into an IRA. The clock begins ticking from the day you receive the check, so make copies of the check and postmarked envelopes for proof.

Averaging

In order to use either 5- or 10-year averaging, you must have a "qualifying" lump-sum distribution. If you don't meet these tests, you can't use averaging although you may still be able to roll your distribution into an IRA.

Under the averaging rules, the distribution must be from a qualified retirement plan, such as a pension, 401(k), or profit-sharing plan, in which you participate for at least five tax years. You cannot use averaging on a distribution from an IRA. Naturally, you must have separated from service with the company making the distribution before you can average it.

Also, you must have separated from service with your employer or have attained age 59 and a half. Also, don't forget that the amount you receive from that lump-sum distribution must equal the full amount due you from all plans of the same type (for example, all profit-sharing-type plans, pension-type plans, and stock bonus-type plans).

Excess Distribution Tax

Further complicating your choices, the IRS has another wrinkle for wealthy taxpayers in the form of a 15 percent additional tax on excess distributions. To find out if you are subject to the tax, add up all of your distributions from pensions and tax-deferred retirement accounts, such as your 401(k), Keogh, IRA, or ESOP. Exclude your Social Security benefits and any money that may represent after-tax contributions you made to the plan. From this amount, subtract $155,000.

The amount that exceeds $155,000 is the amount of your excess distributions.

Annuity Distribution Options

If your company has a defined benefit pension plan, when you eventually retire it will provide several annuity or monthly payment distribution options. Some benefit plans will give you a choice when it comes to withdrawing your pension money: you may receive these in the form of an annuity or you may take a lump-sum distribution.

Most pension plans offer employees a choice of several annuity payments. The basic pension benefit is a single life annuity. The single life annuity is a payment spread over the life of the employee: you'll receive a monthly check for as long as you live. However, after you die, no further payments go to your survivors or your estate.

Many married people prefer what is known as a joint and survivor (J&S) annuity, which pays benefits to you and your survivors as long as either of you live. Generally, your monthly payment will be reduced if you elect a J&S payment in exchange for a guaranteed payment to your survivors. The reduction depends on the age of the survivors: the younger the survivor, the larger the reduction.

Remember, federal law requires that both you and your spouse decide. If you are married and opt for anything other than a 50 percent or higher J&S with your spouse, then your spouse has to consent by law. This consent must be in the form of a notarized waiver that both you and your spouse have signed.

If you and your spouse die when actuaries say you're supposed to, the total dollar amount you will receive is the same for both choices. In other words, both single-life and joint and survivor annuities are designed to be actuarial equivalents.

Annuity versus Lump Sum

If your pension plan provides both annuity and lump-sum payment options, you have a difficult choice to make. Annuities and lump-sum distributions are also designed to be "actuarially equivalent"—either way, you're supposed to get the same amount of money in the end.

However, annuities and lump sums are not equivalent if you die before or after the actuaries say you should. If you die sooner than your actuarial life expectancy, you're actually better off with a lump sum. If you die later, you're better off with an annuity.

Obviously, if you take the lump sum and don't spend it down, you can pass it on to your children or other beneficiaries. Another consideration is the rate of return you will get on your money. When you take an annuity, your company retirement plan takes responsibility for investing the money, and the annuity payments are calculated assuming a particular investment rate of return. For most plans, those assumed rates range between 5 and 8 percent. If you think you can beat this assumed rate of return, opt for a lump-sum payment. Remember, however, there is a risk with annuity payments that you should be aware of: they are not indexed for inflation.

In this lesson, you learned that the risks of a forced separation or early retirement may become a reality. You must figure out what to do with any of your retirement assets that might be invested in either the company or its benefits programs.

INDEX